School Sports and the Law

Term-time ning hours:

E

les. Thu

CRONER © CCH

Croner.CCH Group Limited
145 London Road
Kingston upon Thames
Surrey KT2 6SR
Tel: 020 8547 3333

Published by
Croner.CCH Group Limited
145 London Road
Kingston upon Thames
Surrey KT2 6SR
Tel: 020 8547 3333

First published March 2001

British Library cataloguing in Publication Data. A CIP Catalogue Record for
this book is available from the British Library

ISBN 1 85524 610 4

Printed by Creative Print and Design, Wales

CONTRIBUTORS

AUTHORS

Principal Author

Edward Grayson MA (Oxon)
Is a practising Barrister of the Middle Temple and of the South-Eastern Circuit; Visiting Professor of Sport and the Law at Anglia University; Founding President, British Association for Sport and the Law; and a Fellow of the Royal Society of Medicine. He is a member of Corinthian-Casuals Football Club, MCC, Harlequins, an associate member of the Medical Officers of Schools Association and a member of the Bar Sports Law Group.

Reviewer and Consultant Editor

David Brierley
Studied law at Cambridge University, and has worked with the Professional Association of Teachers (PAT) as their solicitor since 1984. During this time he has advised and represented members from all sectors of education in a wide range of employment issues. His work takes regularly him into schools as well as to courts and Employment Tribunals. David gives talks to schools and governors and is a regular contributor to various Croner.CCH publications.

Authors: Health and Safety, Insurance Chapters

Andrew Deans Solicitor and Partner in Hextall Erskine, London
Andrew read law at Bristol University and qualified as a solicitor in 1980. He has specialised for over 20 years in all aspects of liability insurance and handles a number of insurance schemes for sports associations in both team and individual endeavours. He is also involved in the continuing development of the law relating to acceptance of risk by individuals participating in sport. He has also dealt with a number of major health and safety prosecutions in sport, leisure and in facilities management on behalf of employers, operators of leisure facilities and individuals.

Justin Clayden Assistant Solicitor, Hextall Erskine, London
Justin Clayden qualified as a solicitor in 1997 , having previously been
an Insurance Loss Adjuster for eight years. He has worked closely with
Andrew Deans since joining Hextall Erskine as a trainee solicitor in
1995.

Author: Funding Chapter

Michael J Walker Head, King Edward VII School King's Lynn
The School has received the Sportsmark Award from the Sports Council,
and has been designated by the L.T.A. as a Tennis Development Centre.

Include what government are trying to do to increase sport pp'

INTRODUCTION.

The purpose of this book is to guide all concerned with school sports towards an awareness of the legal responsibilities and regulations which affect coaching training and participation. This guide is a timely reminder of the key legal principles at a time when the funding and strategy for school sports has been bolstered by the Government's recent publication of *A Sporting Future for All*.

A Sporting Future for All was launched by the Chris Smith, the Secretary of State for Culture, Media and Sport, and Sports Minister, Kate Hoey on 5 April 2000. It forms the Government's strategy for sport describing the Government's vision for sport in the 21st century. The publication places particular emphasis on the importance of co-ordinating sport between schools, local clubs and other organisations with a sporting purpose.

On the same day that Chris Smith launched the strategy, Education and Employment Secretary, David Blunkett announced a boost in access to school sports including a five-point plan to help schools develop future sporting stars. The plan is part of *A Sporting Future for All* and includes the following points.

- A fund of £75 million from the Government over two years, with a target of matched funding from the Lottery, for primary schools to provide 300 new, multi-purpose sports and arts facilities for pupils and the wider community.
- The goal of having 110 specialist sports colleges in place by 2003, with close links to the governing bodies of sport, and help for talented young people to tie in with the UK Sports Institute.
- The establishment of up to 600 (subsequently increased to 1000) school sports co-ordinators by Sport England, paid for with Lottery money, to develop more inter-school competitive games.
- Developing more after-school sports and physical education. The £240 million out of hours learning programme funded jointly by the New

Opportunities Fund (£160 million) and the Standards Fund (£80 million) currently supports sports, art, homework and computer clubs outside normal school hours.

- Encouraging world class performance athletes to volunteer to visit a minimum number of schools each year and enabling access to coaching and support for the most talented 14–18 year-olds, as potential elite competitors of the future.

MORI and BMRB surveys for DfEE in 2000 revealed that boys take part in more after school sports than girls. Just over 33% of pupils took part in school organised sports after school or at weekends. The figures went on to indicate that 42% of boys take part but only 28% of girls. Primary school pupils now spend an extra two hours a week at school on extracurricular activities.

The Government's school sports strategy was given continued profile when Chris Smith made a House of Commons statement on the eve of the Parliamentary recess (25 July 2000) on funding for culture and sport. It followed the Chancellor of the Exchequer's announcement a week earlier heralding:

"...a spending review outcome that enables me to give the House details of the highest ever levels of public support for sport and the arts in England".

Mr. Smith stated that:

"...over the next three years, there will be a real terms increase in my department's expenditure of 13.5%".

He made a connection between this statement and his previous reminder of the crucial differences in competitive levels by stating that:

"...as we set out in our recent sports strategy *A Sporting Future For All*, our approach is based both on the regeneration of sport in school and at the grass roots, and on support for our very best sportsmen and sportswomen."

Note: the position of school sports co-ordinators were first proposed in June 1999. They are funded with £60 million of Lottery money from Sport England and the New Opportunities Fund as well as £350,000 in 2000–01 from the DfEE (increasing as the scheme expands).

DIFFERENT DIMENSIONS

The different levels of sporting achievement and endeavour are not incompatible. Indeed, they supplement and complement each other. Without grass roots participation there will not be the opportunity to achieve the status of elite competitor. Yet there are additional dimensions which compound the problem of competing in international arenas. One was observed by the MP Mr. Derek Wyatt, who questioned Chris Smith's statement, mentioned above, as follows:

"May I ask for clarification on one issue on which we have corresponded and that I have mentioned before? There is a weakness in coaching education, sport psychology and sport medicine...given the fantastic achievements of Pete Sampras and of Tiger Woods...could we not devise a new way of recognising, it could be something like an order of merit, outstanding international sporting achievement in this country?"

Mr. Smith's answer led discussion to a key area when he replied:

"...unless we get the grass roots of sport right and in particular encourage sporting participation on a wide scale among young people in school, we will never produce the great athletes and great sportsmen of the future that we will need if we are to make our way internationally."

The need for the Government's sports strategy has been sharpened since its publication in April 2000 by the recent House of Lords Judicial ruling. In this pivotal case, *Phelps v The Mayor and Burgesses of the London Borough of Hillingdon* (The Times 28 July 2000), it was held that one of the LEA's educational psychologists (but not the school) had been negligent and damages of nearly £46,000 were awarded against the LEA. The ruling made clear that skilled education professionals and their employers are placed in the same legal frame as doctors, dentists, nurses and other skilled practitioners in terms of the competent exercise of their specialist skills.

Now that the way has been opened up for claims of negligence in relation to the provision of education — which could be against LEAs and/or a school corporately or (less likely) an individual — there is some concern that such claims might become commonplace, particularly for children with special educational needs.

The stated intention in the Government's *A Sporting Future for All* is to establish 600 (subsequently increased to 1000 in later Government announcements) school sports co-ordinators in communities of greatest need. These are to be based in families of schools linked whenever possible through LEAS to specialist sport colleges. There are to be 110 Specialist Sports Colleges by 2006 (secondary schools with a special focus on physical education and sport, working with the physical education profession to improve the quality and quantity of physical education).

It should be considered to what extent the new category of school sports co-ordinator will share the traditional awareness and knowledge that exists among qualified school sports teacher. Are the co-ordinators always going to be as experienced as their school based colleagues?

The publication of the Government's strategy document also turns the wheel of history full circle. This Government's commitment can be referred back to Lord Hailsham of St. Marylebone who first conceived of government's direct involvement in sport. This was during his occupation as Minister for Science and Technology, in Prime Minister Harold Macmillan's Cabinet during the early 1960s. At that time, as he explained nearly forty years later in *The Door Wherein I Went* (Collins,1975):

> "This particular activity was a minor matter and I thought comparatively little of it at the time since it occurred when other things were occupying my mind (as a cabinet minister for Science Technology in Mr. Macmillan Government)."

Today the popularity and global reach of sporting contests has resulted in it becoming a major constituent element of the entertainment industry which thrives alongside the existence of sporting endeavour at grass roots levels and in schools. It is for the latter purposes that this edition has been prepared. World competition in all sports is a multi-billion pound industry which has grown in part from the roots of physical education. International federations, the Olympic Games, the World Cup are all familiar incarnations of international competition. Many involve more member states than the United Nations. However physical education remains concerned above all else with health, education and the rule of law within and without the laws of fair play in each particular discipline.

FRAGMENTATION

In the United Kingdom fragmentation exists at every level of physical education. There are 13 separate government departments who can be identified as stakeholders (see Chapter 11: Government for a full list). In addition there is the demarcation between the private school sector and LEA maintained schools. There are more than 200 sporting governing bodies threaded throughout the Central Council for Physical Recreation which itself exists alongside Government funded agencies within the United Kingdom created as Sports Councils.

Against this framework *A Sporting Future for All* under the heading of *Sport in Education* (page 29–30 paragraph 7.1–7.7) explains:

"Physical education is an essential part of a broad and balanced curriculum. It enables all young people to develop physical skills, helps personal and social development and has an important impact across the whole curriculum. High quality physical education and school sports well taught by inspirational teachers, qualified coaches and trained adult volunteers also helps make sport and healthy exercise a lifelong habit...All children between the ages of five and sixteen have a statutory entitlement to physical education within the National Curriculum."

A decade later Lord Hailsham wrote in his memoirs *A Sparrow's Flight* in 1990:

"Sport, I believe...is an essential part of education...in my judicial capacity as Lord Chancellor I was part author of a judgement which authenticated the legal status of a fund for Association Football as a charitable trust (*IRC v McMullan, 1980,* A.C.I.). Organised sport is undoubtedly part of our national culture. In mountain climbing, cricket and most of football, in hunting, fishing and game shooting, the British were pioneers in the field of sport as it began in the nineteenth century."

In the same volume he had explained:

"In a sense there is no such thing as sport. There is only a heterogeneous list of pastimes with different governing bodies, different ethics and constantly varying needs."

Four years later be was corroborated from an unexpected legal source. HM Customs and Excise listed 113 non-profit making sports related activities which are exempted from VAT; each has different rules, ethics, varying needs and inevitably different coaching criteria. They appear comprehensively in Chapter 2.

During a Court of Appeal stage as the football charitable trust case was *en route* to the House of Lords, a dialogue between Judge and Counsel produced the following exchange:

Judge: "Are you really saying that physical education is education like Latin and Greek?"

Counsel: "Yes, m'Lord".

An extra dimension exists since the House of Lords ruled in the clutch of cases mentioned earlier (*Phelps v Hillingdon London Borough Council, et al* Times 28 July 2000). These resulted in the general proposition that a local education authority could be vicariously liable for breaches by those whom it employed, including educational psychologists and teachers, of their duties of care towards pupils. Physical education practitioners were not specified but if (and most likely when) the time comes to test the law at this level, the factors covered throughout the book for establishing legal liability are likely to be of key consideration. In more general terms previous cases had already established that persons exercising a particular skill or profession were likely to owe a duty of care in the performance of those skills to those who it could be foreseen would be injured if due skill and care were not exercised. Negligence would be established and if injury or damage could be shown to have been caused by the lack of due care. Such a duty did not depend on the existence of any contractual relationship. The *Phelps* case has made it clear that a teacher, educational psychologist, psychiatrist or a teacher concerned responsible for children with special educational needs (SEN) was such a person. Additionally the ruling may apply to an education officer performing the authority's functions with regards to children with special educational needs. There courts were clear that there was no justification for a blanket immunity for education professionals.

Correspondingly, a teacher or coach with responsibilities for physical education is arguably similarly identifiable and liable for breach of his or her duty of care to those pupils within his or her charge. Those reaffirmed criteria will dominate the whole range of policy driven by *A Sporting Future for All*.

The impact of global sporting entertainment, with international elite competition and international federations for every sporting activity, contrasts sharply with grass roots participation. The contrast is crystallised when *A Sporting Future for All*:

"In too many schools physical education and sport have declined. There has been a loss of playing fields and decline in after school sport and education. We must begin to turn this around. We need to find a new approach that will create substantively long term changes and that support teachers and young people. Our ambition must be to raise the standards of physical education and school sport to match those of the best."

The five point plan with the ultimate goal of providing access for the most talented 14–18 year-olds was linked to involving governing sports bodies, other national institutions including the Sports Council the National Coaching Foundation in addition to the teaching profession.

All children from 5–16 have a statutory entitlement to physical education within the National Curriculum. The National Curriculum for Physical Education specifies attainment targets and programmes of study in relation to Physical Education. These are contained in **The Education (National Curriculum) (Attainment Targets and Programmes of Study in Physical Education) (England) Order 2000** (SI 2000 No.1607). It comprises 44 pages of details structured covering descriptions of eight levels of increasing difficulty, plus a description for exceptional performance above level 8. Each level description describes the types and range of performance that pupils working at that level should characteristically demonstrate with differentials at key stages 1, 2 and 3, leading to key stage 4.

The **Education Act 1996**, s.353b, defines a programme of study as the "matters, skills and processes" that should be taught to pupils of different abilities and maturity during a key stage. They set out what pupils should be taught, and the attainment targets set out the expected standards of pupils performance. Nevertheless the fundamental question which dominates and underlines the whole programme is stated at the outset, that it is:

> "..for schools to choose how they organise their school curriculum to include the programmes of study for physical education".

Yet even before the National Curriculum was formed, the legal requirements for educationalists would always be subject to the principles re-affirmed by the House of Lords in *Phelps v Hillingdon LBB* for the exercising of the overriding duty of care — where failure to exercise due care where there is a foreseeable risk of injury creates liability for negligence.

The Government's *A Sporting Future for All* brings Government involvement with sport and physical education and recreation and leisure comprehensively into line with what Lord Hailsham recognised nearly forty years ago. He describes in *The Door Wherein I Went* (page 207) how:

> "...it occurred during a Cabinet Meeting in which government responsibility for Sport was being discussed. It was being said that properly speaking, responsibility for sport was being shared between quite a number of departments and authorities, education, local government, universities, the services, and all the voluntary bodies dealing with athletics, from the Olympic and Commonwealth Games and League and Cup football at the top to badminton, fives and even chess at the most refined and esoteric end of the spectrum. I pointed out that recreation presented a complex of problems out of which modern government was not wholly free to opt, and which government funds were, in fact, and were likely to continue to be committed in one way or another in coaching, in the provision of playing fields. I waxed eloquent on this subject, talking of the fares for Olympic competitors and many other topics I suggested there was a need, not for a Ministry, but for a focal point under a Minister, for a coherent body of doctrine, perhaps even a philosophy of government encouragement...

INTRODUCTION

> "...this particular activity was a minor matter, and I thought comparatively little of it at the time since it occurred when other things were occupying my mind (as a Cabinet Minister)."

Today that minor matter has evolved into the priorities identified in *A Sporting Future for All*, crafted by the Department for Culture Media and Sport in association with the Department for Education and Employment and "being shared between quite a number of authorities and departments". The legal responsibilities it creates for those who participate within it are the basis for this book.

CHAPTER 1

RESPONSIBILITIES

Who will train the teachers and coaches and to what levels of expertise? For without the correct criteria and an awareness of the safety factors and responsibilities which courts identify, potential dangers will always exist for all concerned within the expanding areas covered by *A Sporting Strategy For All*.

The liability and responsibility for the welfare of students has been further substantiated by the recent House of Lords decision in a clutch of reserved judgment appeals. The House of Lords reaffirmed that a LEA could be vicariously liable for breaches by those whom it employed, including educational psychologists and teachers, of their duties of care towards pupils (*Phelps v Hillingdon LBC*). This principal has existed for decades in physical education and is recorded in *Croner's Head's Legal Guide* in the example of the case of the over-enthusiastic participation by a physical education instructor in a rugby match resulting in an injury to a pupil (*Affuto-Nartoy v Clarke and ILEA*, The Times 9 February 1984); and the case where a student was injured after a teacher acting as umpire in charge of a school cricket game, allowed him to field too close to a batsman (*Barfoot v East Sussex County Council*).

The House of Lords in the *Phelps v Hillingdon LBC* case (The Times 28 July 2000) has explained the following:

"It was well established that persons exercising a particular skill or profession might owe a duty of care in the performance to people who it could be foreseen who would be injured if due skill and care were not exercised and if injury or damage could be shown to have been caused by lack of due care. Such a duty did not depend on the existence of any contractual relationship. An educational psychologist, psychiatrist or a teacher, including a teacher concerned with children having special educational needs, was such a person. So might be an educational officer performing the authority's functions with regard to children with special educational needs. There is no justification for a blanket immunity in their cases."

This decision to uphold the responsibility of a school and its governing bodies to ensure that pupils are appropriately safeguarded from risk that the supervising specialist could have prevented (in this case an undiagnosed dyslexic student) reasserts significant responsibility on the all those in the field of education.

Correspondingly, so too might any coach, physical education teacher or trainer concerned with any pupil injured in his or her care be held responsible for not exercising the appropriate level of care in terms of the activity being taught. All of this is recognised in Derek Wyatt's (MP) claim cited in Chapter 1 that "there is a weakness in coaching education, sport psychology and sport medicine". This statement would seem to suggest therefore that unless and until crucial medical criteria for physical education in schools are recognised, the Government's Sports Strategy is not only flawed, but might it not also be potentially dangerous and damaging to the future health of competitors?

Apart from a passing reference to "ensuring health" no acknowledgement to this essential element appears in the Minister's Spending Review of 25 July 2000.

IN LOCO PARENTIS

The cases in court outlined below demonstrate how the criteria of *in loco parentis* applies to all who are in that relationship with children (ie children in their care), whether school governors, heads, assistant and deputy heads, other school leaders, teachers, referees and even volunteers who undertake responsibilities for whatever purpose.

For over a century the teaching profession has been associated with the concept of *in loco parentis* — literally meaning "in place of parents". For effective and safe coaching to exist it is required that the coach is both aware of and understands the legal responsibilities in addition to possessing technical competence in the sport in question. For example, Judge Barry in Bradford County Court in 1999 in *Casson v MOD* applied against the army personnel who broke the ankle of a then 15 year-old pupil injured during an unstructured mixed boys and girls and adult soldiers football match. The criteria of *in loco parentis*, has a century old longevity stretching back to *Williams v Eady* (1893). On that occasion in a non-sports related case concerning injuries from a chemical substance, Mr. Justice Cave explained the duty with words which have become the guiding definition of the duty. These can be paraphrased for the modern reader as:

"...the person should take such care of the pupil as a careful parent would take care of the same".

The *in loco parentis* criteria dominates the legal responsibilities of teachers. It creates the legal liabilities based upon the duty of care to be exercised where there is foreseeable risk of injury for which a breach will create a liability. The duty will vary with different factual relationships as can be seen reflected in the reported cases.

The borders between teaching and coaching can become blurred and may indeed overlap. However the legal responsibilities of those who are responsible *in loco parentis* remain the same. A number of cases are listed in a legal overview below — some of which involved successful claims against school governing bodies. *Gannon v Rotherham MBC*, concerned a local authority teacher as well as an amateur association, and a further case (*Smolden v Whitworth and Nolan*, 1996 rugby scrum injury) concerned both the governing body and the referee personally.

When considering the overview given below is should be remembered that categories are never closed. The *Affuto-Nartoy* case illustrates the principle of negligently allowing a physically matured teacher to play competitively against a less physically developed pupil. In a further unreported case a host school was found liable for allowing visiting pupils to compete unaware of the hazard created by a concrete dividing line between the rugby field deadball line (behind the goalposts) and a tennis court. A pupil played and was injured because there had been no guidance given of the need to pull up in time to avoid injury.

The supervisory responsibility can span not only the responsibility of the school teacher but also the supervision of playing fields and equipment. Therefore it is important to bear in mind the chain of responsibility and responsible action necessary and how failure at any point may contribute to injury.

Three years after the *in loco parentis* criteria case of 1893 the first road traffic fatality occurred. This has created the current cascade of compensation claims.

The landmark House of Lords decision in *Donoghue v Stevenson*, 1932, is often quoted for its yardstick/criteria for creating and establishing responsibility and liability for civil injury claims generally. Liability exists when a foreseeable risk of injury occurs arising from a breach of the duty of care owed by one person to another. Circumstances vary from case to case. In 1932, which also witnessed the now historic leg theory "bodyline" cricket crisis between England and Australia, the head and governors of Wellingborough Grammar School in Northamptonshire were exonerated from liability in a claim brought for a pupil's injury. An unprecedented striking of a golf ball in a school playground resulted in the ball flying into a school building where it hit the eye of a pupil causing injury. Even with supervision, which was alleged during the case to have been inadequate, the injury was not preventable.

Four years later, however, in 1936, liability was established in the case of a lack of promptitude shown by a teacher in failing to prevent a pupil injury during gymnastic training. The pupil was injured in landing from a vaulting horse in a stumble. The local authority was sued successfully on behalf of the pupil (*Gibbs v Barking Corporation*). Thereafter an unfolding pattern of cases emerge applying to differing circumstances, games and premises. Some of these are reported selectively in Croner's *Heads Legal Guide* and also in *Sport and the Law* (3rd ed) 2000, Grayson and *Ethics Injuries and the Law in Sports Medicine* 1999, Grayson.

Two cases which appear in all three sources cited above merit special attention — although contain elements that should be considered by all school authorities concerned with physical education.

1. The case of the over-enthusiastic rugby player who injured a pupil of lesser physique creating negligent liability — *Affuto-Nartoy v Clarke & ILEA.*
2. The unsuccessful claimant against Bedford School for alleged negligent rugby coaching and absence of insurance cover (*Van Oppen*). This was caused by the parental delay in responding to the school's wish to implement the Rugby Union's acceptance of the Medical Officers for Schools Association (MOSA) recommendation for compulsory insurance in rugby playing schools; and this leads on to the consideration of parents in physical education.

CASES

The cases below are reproduced and updated from *Sport and the Law*, Edward Grayson, 2nd edn 1994, Butterworths, by permission of the publisher (ISBN 0 406 90505 3).

1932	*Langham v Governors of Wellingborough School and Fryer* (1932) 101 LKJB 513, 147 LT 91; 96 JP 236; 30 LGR 276	Facts: Golf ball struck in a school playground hit the eye of a pupil inside a school building causing injury.

Decision: No liability.
Principle: School and staff exonerated from responsibility as the injury could not have been prevented by greater supervision.

1936	*Gibbs v Barking Corporation* All ER 115	Facts: Pupil landed "in a stumble" from a vaulting horse during gymnastic training, suffering personal injury.

Decision: Local authority liable.
Principle: Accident caused by a lack of promptitude by teacher to prevent the stumble when or after vaulting.

1938	*Gillmore v London County Council* 4 All ER 331, 55 TLR 95, 159 LT 615	Facts: A fee-paying adult, participating in a physical training class, slipped on a polished floor while wearing rubber soles (suitable for dancing but not physical exercise).

Principle:
1. Council failed in the duty to provide a floor which was reasonably safe in circumstances, thereby creating danger beyond the usual degree.
2. *Violenti non fit injuria* defence rejected because of absence of consent to risk of this added danger beyond ordinary hazard lawfully practised.

1939	*Clark v Bethnal Green Corp* 55 TLR 519	Facts: Child at swimming bath let go suddenly of a springboard to which she had been clinging, thereby disrupting preparation to jump from it by another child who suffered injury. Decision: No liability Principle: Action not capable of anticipation, irrespective of adequacy of supervision, for which evidence was equivocal and not definitive.
1939	*Barfoot v East Sussex CC* (unreported: Croner's *Heads Legal Guide*, and *Caught in Court*, John Scott, 1989)	Facts: School pupil injured when fielding at cricket, under supervision of teacher also acting as umpire. Evidence conflict between: 1. Plaintiff pupil's claim of placed at "silly mid-on". 2. Defendant's (the teacher) claim of placing at "square leg" location (at right angles to wicket) and the plaintiff moving close to batsman of own accord. Decision: Liability proved. Principle: Umpire duties precluded exercise of sufficient supervisory care by teacher in charge. They conflicted with the need to prevent the pupil being very considerably less than ten yards from the wicket (as judged by court). This was a dangerous situation and resulted in the judgement of a failure to exercise the care which the law required from a teacher in charge of a pupil in these circumstances.

Scott's (1989) researches revealed that the trial judge, Justice Humphreys awarded damages after "deciding with fear and trembling and with as much courage as I can assume", to disagree with the expert testimony of the Sussex and England all-round player, Maurice Tate.

1947	*Ralph v LCC* (1947) 63 TLR 546, CA, 111 JP 548	Facts: School game of "touch" played in room with insufficient space and one participant placed hand unwittingly through glass partition causing injury. Decision: Liability proved. Principal: Reasonable and prudent father would have contemplated possibility of such an accident.
1968	*Beamont v Surrey CC*(1968) 66 LGR 580, 112 SJ 704	Facts: Horseplay during school break caused foreseeable injury of a pupil's eye from discarded elastic rope because of breakdown in usually adequate school supervision. Decision: Liability proved. Principle: 1. Reasonable prudent parent principle (above) not applied to headmaster of school with 900 pupils. 2. Duty breached, to take all reasonable and proper steps to prevent injury between pupils, bearing in mind known propensities of boys or girls between ages 11 and 18.

1981	*Moore v Hampshire CC(1981) 80 LGR 481 C*	Facts: 12 year-old pupil with dislocated hip and unfit for physical training of which teacher advised. Teacher was wrongfully persuaded that permission authorised. Disability caused awkward movement resulting in injury. Decision: Liability proved. Principle: Double failure to: (a) observe awkward movements (b) to supervise properly with regards to the needs of disabled child.
1981	*Tracey Moore v Redditch and Bromsgrove Gymnast Club* (unreported: but given to emphasises the value of insurance for victim and insured)	Facts: 18 year-old gymnast injured when using trampoline facilities in gymnasium during period of supervision at gymnasium club. Decision: Out of court settlement. Principle: No admission of liability on negligence allegation. Claim: £350000. Insurance policy ceiling at £250000. Settlement £250000, with denial on liability that supervision was inadequate.
1984	*Affuto-Nartoy v Clarke and ILEA* Times, 9 February 1984	Facts: 15 year-old pupil injured during school rugby game by a high tackle from teacher during instructional period, without any unfair play issue. Decision: Liability proved. Principle: Teacher in a momentary lapse, forgot that the pupils were of a lesser physique.

1985	*Condon v Basi* 2 All ER 453	Facts: Soccer player injured by foul play in club match sued for wrongful assault and negligence in claim for broken leg. Decision: Liability proved. Principle: Negligence upheld in Court of Appeal because the duty owed by one competitor to another to play according to the rules was breached on this occasion by violent foul play.
1988	*Van Oppen v Clerk to the Bedford Charity Trustees* 3 All ER 389, CA	Facts: Pupil injured by rugby tackle but not insured. Decision: Negligence not proved and alleged failure to insure rejected. Principle: Evidence of no negligence. No duty to insure equivalent to non-parental duty to insure.
1991	*Gannon v Rotherham MBC* Halsbury's Monthly Review (1991) 91/1717	Facts: Pupil recovered damages against the supervising teacher and the governing body for broken neck sustained in swimming bath injury. Decision: Liability proved. Principle: Supervision and guidance provided has been inadequate. The case of Gannon in 1991, arose from a swimming teachers liability in a swimming pool owed by a neighbouring local authority; and in another injury suffered during a visiting rugby schoolboy's collision with a concrete barrier. An out of court settlement was achieved.
1993	*Morrell v Owen* Times, 14 December 1993	Facts: Disabled wheelchair athlete injured by unsafe discus thrower. Decision: Negligence proved.

		Principle: Higher duty of care owned to athletes under disability than to able-bodied participants.
1996	*Smolden v Whitworth and Nolan* Times, 18 December, CA	Facts: Under-19 rugby colts player paralysed during a collapsed scrum, in breach of rules of the game. Decision: Negligence proved. Principle: Breach of duty of care through ignorance of rules of game.
1998	*Williams v Rotherham LEA* Times, 6 August 1998	Facts: Pupil forced to join PE lesson notwithstanding injured ankle. Decision: Negligence proved. Principle: Known aggravation of pre-existing injurous condition exacerbated physically injured ankle.
1998	*R v David Calton* Yorkshire Post, 29 September 1998	Facts: Broken jaw suffered in rugby match between two leading Yorkshire private schools. Decision: Conviction following Crown Court Prosecution. Sentence: 12 months at Young Offenders Institution. Principle: Law of land does not stop at touchline, even for young offenders.
1999	*Casson v MOD* Bradford Telegraph, Yorkshire Post 1999	Facts: Broken leg from negligent tackle by member of Army, when in loco parentis to plaintiff. Decision: Damages awarded. Principle: Gross reckless negligence.

The law does not require absolute safety. Teachers and coaches are not required to attempt to take away all the risk — particularly where they may be inherent in the enjoyment of the game according to the accepted rules and standards. They are however required to follow safe practice and minimise risk.

The British Association of Advisors and Lecturers in Physical Education (BAALPE) explain this in the introduction to the millennium edition of its guidance *Safe Practice in Physical Education*.

"Every tragedy or accident that occurs serves to highlight the importance of safe practice and the need to learn lessons and adopt procedures that will minimise the likelihood of a recurrence of such incidents. More importantly careful forethought and preparation will help prevent such occurrences."

The purpose of the BAALPE guidance is to advise on safe practice across a range of activities which may be included in physical education programmes and to inform teachers on aspects of good and accepted safe practice consistent with decided cases. There is more information on these issues in the health and safety management chapter.

CHAPTER 2

DIVERSITY OF SPORTING ACTIVITIES

FEATURES OF *A SPORTING FUTURE FOR ALL*

The key features of the Government's strategy for sport *A Sporting Future for All* as already mentioned are:

- A fund of £75 million from the Government over two years, with a target of matched funding from the Lottery, for primary schools to provide 300 new, multi-purpose sports and arts facilities for pupils and the wider community.
- The goal of having 110 specialist sports colleges in place by 2003, with close links to the governing bodies of sport, and help for talented young people to tie in with the UK Sports Institute.
- The establishment of up to 600 (subsequently increased to 1000) school sports co-ordinators by Sport England, paid for with Lottery money, to develop more inter-school competitive games.
- Developing more after-school sports and physical education. The £240 million out of hours learning programme funded jointly by the New Opportunities Fund (£160 million) and the Standards Fund (£80 million) currently supports sports, art, homework and computer clubs outside normal school hours.
- Encouraging world class performance athletes to volunteer to visit a minimum number of schools each year and enabling access to coaching and support for the most talented 14–18 year olds, as potential elite competitors of the future.

COACHES AND COACH CO-ORDINATORS

Coaches must always remain aware of their responsibilities to preserve the welfare of their pupils, particularly as they are dealing with vulnerable participants. It is essential to exercise different levels of care and control between different disciplines dependent of the requirements for the safe conduct of the activity.

Already described earlier is the issue of the physical maturity of the participants. The is important where discrepancies between the sizes of participants and unequal physical maturity may impact on their safety. Of equal consideration is the physical maturity of all the participants and how this will affect their ability (ie the ability of all the participants) to perform to expected standards. In addition there is of course the issue of mental maturity. Junior participants cannot be expected to perform in a way that will always take due consideration of both their safety and that of others.

In a leading case concerning one coach's responsibilities for disabled competitor athletes, *Morrell v Owen*(Times 14 December 1993), Mr Justice Mitchell cited the coach to the successful disabled athletes association, after an injury was sustained caused by a discuss thrown on the other side of a net curtain.

Describing the (male in this case) coach's status he said: "His word is law. He is akin to a God. What he says goes." He went on to say of Mr Taylor, the coach:

"The coach is the man the athletes are entitled to rely on for their procedures. Safety first has to mean first not later, hoping meanwhile that common-sense alone will ensure it."

Mr. Justice Mitchell readily acknowledged that anyone coaching at the level the athletes concerned were competing at was entitled to expect of the participants knowledge of the safety requirements in relation to his own or her own sport. However, very particularly in any judgement he pointed out that it could be that athletes from one discipline did not fully understand what happened in another. We should consider how this decision for mature athletes is equally applicable for coaching children at school level with the additional consideration as outlined above of the physical and mental maturity of the participants. In this judgement Mr. Justice Mitchell made quite clear that having sat and listened to the evidence over a number of days he was quite convinced this was the case here. At the end of his judgement he made this point:

"You cannot simply apply normal safety standards to disabled sports activities. The disabled are not always ambulant. In any event movement can take longer and there will always be a range of disabilities involved."

A contrary policy was expressed by an expert from the unsuccessful defendant's professional association. The expert said:

"At this standard I would expect an athlete's knowledge of safety matter to be absolute and fully capable of conducting himself in a safe way. I see no need to warn athletes at that level of their own safety. It is preaching the obvious. The more you do that the less notice they tend to take."

This viewpoint was rejected by the judge and doubtless will be by all concerned with the safe organisation and conduct of physical education.

Participants in activities should undoubtedly be aware of the rules of the sports in which they are competing. The *Morrell* case makes it clear that you cannot apply the same standards where the participants may have physical or mental disabilities. In addition all participants, and particularly juniors, may not be aware of their limitations or the potential that they will not meet the requirements of the discipline.

It is in this area of concern that the Government strategy of *A Sporting Future for All* will stand or fall. The introduction states:

"The strategy does not touch on every issue that is topical in sport today. But it does seek to identify the best ways to bring about all round improvement and to initiate co-ordinated and purposeful action."

The following section *Sport in Education* explains:

"We will work with the physical education profession to help teachers improve the quantity and quality of physical education and sport in schools. We believe that physical education is an essential part of a broad and balanced curriculum and are determined that this should be a positive and enjoyable experience for all young people."

Subsequently (page 16) the document states that:

"Coaching is central to the development of excellence. The coach has to be able to co-ordinate and manage other coaches, sports scientists and sports medicine personnel, deal with media and provide consistent mentoring and supports for their performers."

Further affirmation of the central importance of effective coaching is made as follows (page 43, paragraph 93):

"Coaches play a central role in the development of sport at every level. Much good work has been done in coaching education in the UK but we wish to see greater use of new technology to improve accessibility of coach education and a concerted effort to improve the quality and quantity in all sports."

This ideal in turn is followed by the stated aim to ensure that future development is undertaken with all the relevant key agencies and that a review of coaching and the education of coaches is part of this process.

In every category of coaching there must be the central awareness of the potential risks and adverse outcomes which are possible and for which a breach creates a liability. This can be reaffirmed by considering the cases of *Affuto-Nartoy v Clarke and ILEA* (rugby) and the *Barfoot v East Sussex CC* (cricket) cases mentioned in the previous chapter. Every activity has its own coaching structure and must operate within the duty of care.

Equally significant for the problem of safe and effective coaching are two features at different ends of the physical education spectrum. The first is that the bulk of primary schools are unable to provide specialist physical education teachers; and at the other end of the spectrum the question emerges of who will train and what is taught for the new category of coach co-ordinator mentioned in *A Sporting Future for All*.

The role of school sports co-ordinator was first proposed in June 1999. The co-ordinators are to be funded with National Lottery money from Sport England and the New Opportunities Fund as well as money allocated by the DfEE (which is set to increase as the scheme expands. There is of course the important questions to be answered of who will train the new co-ordinators and what is to be by them. Overriding and underpinning their performance standards are the criteria identified in the case of *Phelps v Hillingdon LBC* where the ruling made it clear that skilled education professionals and their employers are placed in the same legal frame as doctors, dentists, nurses and other skilled practitioners in terms of the competent exercise of their specialist skills.

> "Persons enjoying a particular skill or profession might owe a duty of care in the performance to people who it could be foreseen would be injured if due skill and care were not exercised and if injury or damage could be shown to have been exercised by the lack of due care."

The *Phelps* case was one of four test cases in which the House of Lords gave its judgement which raised the question of whether an LEA could be vicariously liable for breaches by those it employed, including educational psychologists and teachers of their duty of care towards pupils with special educational needs (SEN). Three of the test cases concern pupils with dyslexia and the fourth test case concerned a pupil with muscular dystrophy. The cases were *Phelps v London Borough of Hillingdon Council, Anderton v Clwyd County Council, Gower v Bromley London Borough Council* and *Jarvis v Hampshire County Council*. There is currently no remedy in damages if an LEA is in breach of its statutory duty in respect of its assessment and treatment of a pupil with special educational needs.

The unanimous decision of the seven Law Lords was that if the system fundamentally failed a child in his or her education then the child had the same right to seek compensation as in the case of any other professional, such as a doctor, lawyer or financial advisor. Breaches of the duty of care towards pupils could include a failure to diagnose dyslexia or to provide appropriate education for pupils with SEN. The House of Lords added that failure to mitigate the adverse consequences of a congenital defect, such as dyslexia, could constitute "personal injuries to a person" and therefore warrant damages.

Lord Slynn said in his judgement that it was well established that persons exercising a particular skill or profession might owe a duty of care to people who it could be foreseen would be injured if due skill and care were not exercised. If injury or damage could be shown to have been caused by the lack of care there could be a valid claim. He added that he was very conscious of the need to be cautious in recognising such a duty of care where so much was discretionary and that it is important that those engaged in the provision of educational services under the Education Acts should not be hampered by the imposition of such a liability.

The conclusion of the judgement was to reject the absolute statement that an LEA "owes no common law duty of care...in the exercise of the powers...relating to children with SEN" under the **Education Act 1981**.

This case equally applies to physical education and therefore physical education teachers and the new category of coach co-ordinator.

Many of the cases identified in Chapter 2 have established vicarious liability against a local authority: for example *Affuto-Nartoy v Clark and ILEA* (rugby) and *Barfoot v East Sussex CC* (cricket). The *Phelps v Hillingdon BC* House of Lords decision re-emphasises what is illustrated by the *Affuto* case and *Barfoot* decisions that vicarious liability exists for the negligent activities of those acting within the course of their employment.

DIVERSITY OF ACTIVITIES

As stated earlier there are 113 different categories of sporting activity that are exempted for VAT purpose. Consider this potential multiplicity of sporting activites against the requirements of the attainment targets stated in the National Curriculum (SI 2000/1607). The curriculum document states:

"It is for schools to choose how they organise their school curriculum to include the programme of study for physical education."

Schools must be aware that every one of the activities provided at school require different techniques in coaching and that standards must be maintained to ensure safety in the exercise of a particular activity. The risk element is illimitable for injury, and will be reflected in insurance premiums specified in the Insurance Chapter and the statistics for sports related injuries in Chapter 7.

The key factor in cases concerning sporting activities will be the extent to which the risks were foreseeable. Remembering that the definition for negligence is that there is a duty of care with a foreseeable risk of injury likely to cause consequential damage and harm (*Donaghue v Stevenson*). Detailed information about risk assessment is contained in the chapter on Health and Safety.

VAT Exempted UK Sporting Activities

The following list is those UK sports activities which quality for exemption as non-profit making activities for VAT purposes (though many will be rarely available in school!). These are illustrative of the range of sporting activities available to young people for which differing coaching services may be required (HM Customs and Excise VAT 701/45/94).

Akido	Dragon Boat Racing	Lawn Tennis	Snowboarding
American Football	Equestrian	Life Saving	Softball
Angling	Exercise and Fitness	Luge	Squash
Archery	Fencing	Modern Pentathlon	Street Hockey
Arm Wrestling	Field Sports	Motor Cycling	Rugby Union
Association Football	Fives	Motor Sports	Sailing/Yachting

Athletics	Flying	Mountaineering	Sand/Land Yachting
Badminton	Gaelic Football	Movement and Dance	Shinty
Ballooning	Gliding	Netball	Shooting
Baseball	Golf	Orienteering	Skateboarding
Basketball	Gymnastics	Parachuting	Sub-Aqua
Baton Twirling	Handball	Petanque	Sumo Wrestling
Biathlon	Hang/para Gliding	Polo	Surf Life Saving
Bicycle Polo	Highland Games	Pony Treking	Surfing
Billiards	Hockey	Pool	Swimming
Bobsleigh	Horse Racing	Quoits	Table Tennis
Boccia	Hovering	Rackets	Taekwondo
Bowls	Hurling	Racquetball	Tang Soo Do
Boxing	Ice Hockey	Rambling	Tenpin Bowling
Camogie	Ice Skating	Real Tennis	Trampolining
Canoeing	Jet Ski	Roller Hockey	Triathlon
Caving	Ju Jitsu	Roller Skating	Tug of War
Chinese Martial Arts	Judo	Rounders	Unihoc
Cricket	Kabaddi	Rowing	Volleyball
Croquet	Karate	Rugby League	Water Skiing
Crossbow	Kendo	Skiing	Weightlifting
Curling	Korfball	Skipping	Wrestling
Cycling	Lacross	Snooker	Yoga

VAT in relating to non-profit making sport may appear far removed from the Government's sports strategy. Its impact can be seen directly on all who wish to benefit from potential charitable status arising from the House of Lords decisions on sports related educational and recreational Charities Act situations. The case of *IRC v McMullan* (1981 AC 1) confirmed and emphasised that physical education is legally regarded as educational and eligible for charitable status. The taxation advantages are therefore of importance to sports clubs and to schools for the potential use they might derive from partnership with clubs and other owners of facilities.

CHAPTER 3

PARENTS AND PUPILS

HUMAN RIGHTS ACT

The **Human Rights Act 1998** received the Royal Assent on 9 November 1998 and came into force on 2 October 2000. On that very important date the *European Convention on Human Rights* became incorporated into the UK law and UK citizens are now able to enforce their rights under the convention in domestic courts, instead of having to go to the European Court of Human Rights in Strasbourg.

The European Convention on Human Rights was adopted in 1950 and the European Court of Human Rights was set up in 1959 to decide whether in particular cases rights under the Convention had been infringed. UK citizens have been able to petition the court since 1966. There have been a number of cases against the UK concerning educational matters. One particularly important case, *Campbell and Cosans v UK*, dealt with corporal punishment in schools. Other cases have dealt with parental rights in relation to special education needs. Non-education cases have included cases about the rights of individuals in the criminal process and a recent case challenging telephone tapping.

The Convention includes prohibition of torture, slavery and forced labour and the right to liberty. It also includes basic rights for the individual that should be present in a democratic society. Public authorities have a legal duty to act consistently with the Convention rights. The definition of a public authority in the Act is not confined to central and local government bodies such as the DfEE, Ofsted, the GTC and local education authorities. The definition also includes the police, the courts and tribunals. Private bodies whose work includes functions of a public nature are public authorities. This means that governing bodies of maintained schools are treated as public authorities.

The Act has changed the landscape of the English Legal system; but so far as education and in particular physical education are affected, it re-interprets what has existed for over half a century under s.76 of the **Education Act 1944** (now s.9 of the **Education Act 1996**) which provides (with my emphasis):

> "In the exercise and performance of all powers and duties conferred and imposed on them by this Act (the secretary of State) and local education authorities shall have regard to the (1996: general) principal that, so far as is compatible with the provision of efficient instruction and training and the avoidance of unreasonable public expenditure, pupils are to be educated in accordance with the wishes of their parents."

Section 99 of that same 1944 Act (now s.497 of the **Education Act 1996**) contains a limited sanction for enforcing this section: and s.6 of 1996 Act provides a network of criteria for contributing to the exercise of parental preference. To date the cases which have arrived in the English courts under the sections have never touched upon physical education and sport. With the financial prizes now in reach from all levels of recreational activities attempts can be anticipated by parents and pupils too to activate the Right to Education under Article 2, Protocol 1:

> "No person shall be denied the right to education. In the exercise of any functions which it assumes in relation to education of teaching. The state shall respect the rights of parents to ensure such education and teaching in conformity with their own religious or philosophical convictions."

The UK has accepted this Article but with the reservation that it is implemented only so far as it is compatible with the provision of efficient instruction and training and the avoidance of unreasonable public expenditure. This wording appears in the **Education Act 1996** as a caveat to the duty to provide education in accordance with parental wishes.

To date none of the cases which have arrived in any of the courts exercising jurisdiction under the Education Acts have impinged upon the physical education and sports scene in terms of parental preference. So far from anticipating that this will remain undisturbed, circumstances involving positive wished for participation in one or more particular activity, or negatively for withdrawal from another can easily be visualised.

Article 8 of the Human Rights convention guarantees a right to respect for private and family life and Article 9 guarantees the freedom to practice one's religion. Parental choice was stimulated by religious preferences. However physical education preferences may become more powerfully communicated with the obvious long term financial available to elite competitors.

When deciding issues which directly affect individuals, such as employment issues or admission or exclusion cases, a governing body will be duty bound to act in line with Convention rights. Governors must consider any arguments and representations, based on the Convention rights, which are put to them.

At first glance the governing body of an independent school is not a public authority. However there have been cases when independent schools have been challenged by judicial review on the basis that they are carrying out functions of a public nature.

Qualifications to the Rights

Most of the Convention Rights contain qualifications in order to balance rights by responsibilities. For example there is a qualification to Article 10 (right to freedom of expression) as follows:

> The exercise of these freedoms, since it carries with it duties and responsibilities, may be subject to such formalities, conditions, restrictions or penalties as are prescribed by law and are necessary in a democratic society, in the interests of national security, territorial integrity or public safety, for the prevention of disorder or crime, for the protection of health or morals, for the protection of the reputation or rights of others, for preventing the disclosure of information received in confidence, or for maintaining the authority and impartiality of the judiciary.

There are similar qualifications to Articles 8, 9 and 11.

Schools do carry out a public service so the Act will be relevant to many parts of school life and decisions taken by governors will be scrutinised against convention rights. If a breach of convention rights is established, a court or tribunal can grant such remedy as it considers just and appropriate. There can also be a declaration of incompatibility if the court decides that UK legislation is incompatible with convention rights.

OTHER SPORTING CONSIDERATIONS

The Government's proposed intention to extend the **Disability Discrimination Act 1996** to cover school pupils could open up a further avenue for exploration. The Special Educational Needs and Disability Bill which has actioned this proposal will be enacted in 2001. The DfEE recognised that physical education and sport has an important role in the education of pupils with Special Educational Needs both in special schools and maintained schools. The duty of care for SEN pupils is higher one than for those outside this category because they will need extra care and the judgement in *Morrel v Owen 1993* in favour of a disabled wheelchair archer cited earlier in Chapter 3 is of particular relevance.

Separate and apart from these statutory parameters, or rather within them, are the complex range of physical maturity, emotional maturity, sex differences as well as the potential for child abuse and bullying, all of which are likely to emerge for consideration under the earlier United Kingdom Education Acts and now the Human Rights Act scenario. These must inevitably push back the frontiers of parent, pupil and physical education relationships.

It is the duty of the parent of a child of compulsory school age to ensure that he or she receives effective full-time education. Section 37 of the **Education Act 1996** states that the education should be suitable to the age, ability and aptitude and to any special educational needs that the pupil may have "either by regular attendance at school or otherwise".

Schooling is not compulsory but education is. This means that parents may decide not to register a child at a maintained or registered independent school and may make other arrangements for the child to be educated including education at home. (Education Otherwise is an organisation which gives parents information and advice on educating children otherwise than at school.) If they decide "otherwise" and provide education at home, this must be provided in a way that satisfies LEA inspectors that the education is suitable and efficient. LEAs may provide a home tutor for handicapped, sick or excluded pupils.

Parents whose children are on a school register have a duty to ensure that their children attend regularly and if they fail to do so they may be found to be guilty of an offence (s.444 of the **Education Act 1996**). Absence due to an "unavoidable" cause is not an offence but parents have no right to authorise the absence of a registered pupil of compulsory school age; this may only be done by the school. The general legal principles applicable to school attendance; potential vicarious liability with specific statutory rights now further enshrined in the Human Rights legislation for education generally.

The Human Rights legislation re-emphasises the earlier entitlement of choice for physical education. If pressed too far however it can be damaging to the health of children in the manner explained clearly in a

Lancet commentary at the time of the 1996 Atlanta Olympic Games (Vol. 348:10 August 1996), from a French source:

"Most top level athletes start their careers as adolescents. The problems associated with high level sport include exercise inducing delay in growth, complex musculoskeletal injury, side effects of performance enhancing drugs and psychological damage. They readily become victims of parental ambitions, the demands of trainers and totalitarian control of the federation of their sport. Training damages adolescents social life, psychological development and physical health."

For this reason the responsibility of the coach should include safeguards against the over ambitious aspirations of parental wishes for their children's physical development.

Two graphic modern examples of parental and family decisions being exercised for the direction of the pupil's sporting potential exist in the family decisions of the education for Will Carling and Bobby Charlton. The future England Rugby captain's parents selected Sedburgh school for its rugby playing traditions against other potential choices. The grandfather of Sir Bobby Charlton and his primary school head at Ashington, Co. Durham, influenced his switch of scholarship from Morpeth Grammar School (with a rugby playing tradition) to Bedlington Grammar School, where his soccer playing skills were allowed to flourish to their present repute.

Neither of these decisions were taken under the then available provisions of s.76 of the **Education Act 1944** (now s.9 of the 1996 Act). The 1996 Act provides with qualifications "pupils are to be educated in accordance with the wishes of their parents." This has received little attention generally to date even when disputes have arisen about parent's wishes and choices particularly with physical and temperament incompatibilities with various physical education activities: eg size and gender for particular team games. All this may change however with the **Human Rights Act 1998**. Article 2, Protocol 1, provides for the right to education and that "the State shall respect the rights of parents to ensure education and teaching in conformity to their own religious and philosophical convictions".

Parental influence in physical education can be identified both beneficially and adversely. The overuse syndrome has been tackled graphically and famously in the American publication by Joan Regan, *Little Girls in Pretty Boxes: The Making and Breaking of Elite Gymnasts and Figure Skaters.*

Finally parental rights also exist for withdrawal from physical education on health grounds (see *Moore v Hampshire 1981*). The child was provided with a note for excluding from physical education in this case gymnastics but the teacher was over persuaded by the child with injurious consequences and legal liability. In that context the physical education sector of any school should be prepared for contingencies and limited capacities. Pre-existing ill health, such as asthma and any other limiting condition, must be considered as if ignored may result in a serious incident and could create a legal liability due to prior knowledge of the potentially disabling incapacity.

CHAPTER 4

OUT OF SCHOOL ACTIVITIES

It has long been recognised that there are considerable educational benefits to be derived from out-of-school activities and that the range of such activities continues to grow. The personal and social development of pupils can be considerably enhanced by such activities.

LEAs are likely to maintain guidance regarding the conduct of such trips and ensuring the health safety and welfare of pupils, teachers and others involved. LEAs should be consulted for their guidance.

It should be noted that the majority of visits are undertaken without incident. The organisation of such visits is frequently characterised by high levels of planning and safety considerations. However the Lyme Bay Dorset canoeing tragedy, or skiing fatalities and rock climbing litigation have all highlighted high risk areas fraught with potential danger if allowed to develop without appropriate and adequate training, supervision and skills or special expertise. Parents and school staff are increasingly concerned about maintaining and improving standards.

The Lyme Regis disaster ended in criminal prosecutions with corporate and personal criminal liability proved *R v Kite, Stoddart and OLL Ltd*, Winchester Crown Court, 1994. The prosecution for corporate manslaughter was successful partly because the company was operated by one man who could clearly be identified as its controlling mind. It was established that the individual had sufficient *mens rea* to be convicted of manslaughter. The conviction of the company followed automatically from this.

The **Activity Centres (Young Persons' Safety) Act 1995** and the **Adventure Activities Licensing Regulations 1996** were introduced in response to the Lyme Bay tragedy. The legislation was enacted to introduce a licensing regime for commercial organisations providing specified activities to young people under 18, to ensure that the adventure activity industry was regulated to ensure a high standard of safety. A guidance document exists *Health and Safety of Pupils on Educational Visits* which is essential for reference purposes. This report comes to 62 pages enshrining comprehensive guidance, four pages of source organisations.

The Lyme Bay disaster manslaughter prosecutions and other convictions identify the crucial need for supervision at all times with the exercising of specialist skills and control. Liability has been established for negligent rock climbing and thereby comparably applicable to outward bound and all high risk areas and activities.

The **Management of Health and Safety at Work Regulations 1999** (made under the **Health and Safety at Work, etc Act 1974**) place a duty on employers to conduct a risk assessment in order to ensure that hazards are quantified and thus risks removed or minimised by appropriate control measures. Employees must be informed of these measures. Furthermore employees must act and co-operate with the employer to maintain both their and others health and safety. This includes undertaking activities in accordance with training and informing the employer of significant risks. In addition the responsible adult has, of course, the duty of acting *in loco parentis* when supervising pupils.

Heads should ensure regulations and LEA/school guidance is complied with. Necessary measures to minimise risk and ensure child protection should be in place before any visit begins. This may involve additional staff training. The group leader must be competent and experienced enough to manage the visit safely. Similarly and of key importance is that the leader or another teacher should be competent to instruct the activity and be familiar with the location. Therefore planning time will be crucial to ensure the following has been observed:

- ratios of supervisors to pupils
- LEA/governing body approval
- parental consent
- medical or other special needs arrangements
- travel plans
- insurance
- school and visit party contact details
- agreed emergency procedures
- copy of parent and next of kin contact details held by group leader
- contingency plans for late return.

The group leader's overall responsibility as approved by the head or governing body should include:
- prior approval for visit; following LEA/governing body procedures
- defining roles of other staff on visit including a deputy leader
- child protection
- first aid provision
- planning
- briefing group staff and parents
- constant review of arrangements to maintain safety and welfare
- ensuring sufficient information to assess suitability of pupils for the visit
- ensure supervisor/pupil rations are appropriate
- ensure copies of information outlined in paragraph above are kept.

Supervision is the key for all out of school activities and proportionality and relativity to age groups are essential assessments in advance, with medical insurance arrangements concurrent. The ratio of supervisors will be based on the following factors:
- age and ability of group
- SEN or other medical needs
- nature of activity
- experience of supervisors
- duration of journey
- type of accommodation
- competence of staff
- requirement of organisation to be visited
- behaviour and competence of pupils
- first aid cover.

Published guideline examples include the following:

General guidance

years 1–3	years 4–6	years 7+
1 adult per 6 pupils (higher for under 5s)	1 adult per 10–15 pupils (per 12 pupils for swimming)	1 adult per 15–20 pupils

The following flowchart (taken from DfEE guidance, *Health and Safety of Pupils on Educational Visits*) provides a summary of the planning process.

Outline proposals to head teacher or governing body, or LEA, seeking approval in principle. Proposals might include:
- visit objectives
- likely date, duration and venue
- pupil group, staffing
- resources, estimate of costs

Note: proposals for longer visits may need making in advance of the start of the relevant academic year

Planning:
- contact venue, is it suitable for the group?
- what are the transport options?
- who would lead the group and who would help to supervise?
- who would pay for the visit
- risk assessment, exploratory visit

Substantive proposal to head teacher, or governing body or LEA
- details of dates, risk assessment, emergency procedures, transport, insurance, costs, group membership, staffing

Shorter visits:
- obtain approval and parental consent for visits involving years 1–3 or for day visits
- inform parents as necessary of shorter routine visits
- brief pupils
- go on visit monitoring the risk at all times

Residential and abroad:
- obtain approval to prepare the visit subject to satisfactory preparation

Final preparation:
- information to and from parents; briefing evening (meet supervisors); brief pupils; deposits/full payments by parents
- obtain final approval from LEA or governors, and parental consent
- go on visits monitoring risks at all times

Evaluate

It should be noted that involving pupils in planning and organising will allow them to be better informed and more able to prevent harm occurring through insufficient appreciation of hazards. Pupil consideration of health and safety can be built into the educational context of activities.

As has already been mentioned, in addition to first aid arrangements it is important to be aware of any additional health needs of pupils. Parents should be asked to supply information sufficient to ensure the welfare of pupils including information such as:

- medical conditions
- emergency contact details including GP details
- information on medication
- agreements on administering of medication
- ability to cope away from home
- allergy and phobias
- dietary requirements
- other equipment or aids
- transport issues where mobility is an issue.

The license status of providers for adventure activities can be checked at the Adventurous Activities Licensing Authority, 17 Lambourne Crescent, Llanishen, Cardiff CF4 5GG. Tel: 01222 755 715. Fax: 01222 755 757. Web: www.aala.org

The following table lists activities that need a license when commercial companies sell them to be undertaken by young persons under 18 years of age.

Note: many activities not mentioned here will be covered by health and safety legislation alone.

Caving	All instances where specialist equipment is required.
Climbing	Including sea-level traversing, abseiling, scrambling, climbing man made structure, etc which required specialist equipment or expertise
Trekking	On foot, horseback, bicycle, ski, skates, sledge, over ground above 600 metres when it would require 30 minutes or more to reach an accessible road or refuge. Off-piste skiing requires a licence
Watersports	Sailing, canoeing, kayaking, rafting, windsurfing where any part of waters is 50 metres from the nearest land (rowing is exempt).

CHAPTER 5

FACILITIES AND EQUIPMENT

The **Workplace (Health, Safety and Welfare) Regulations 1992** (SI 1992 No.3004), as amended in part by **Construction (Health, Safety and Welfare) Regulations 1996** (SI 1996 No.1592) require employers and persons who are in charge of work premises to maintain the workplace and the equipment used therein in an efficient state. They must be kept in good repair and in efficient working order. Regulations cover, among others, ventilation, lighting, temperature and cleanliness as well as the organisation of traffic routes for pedestrians, sanitary conveniences and facilities for rest.

LEAs are careful that apparatus is only used by or under the supervision of qualified people. The teacher who ignores this, and the Head who has knowledge of the infraction, may be negligent.

DES Administrative Memorandum No. 2/68 *Physical Education Apparatus in Schools and Colleges* draws attention to the dangers of high rebound apparatus, especially in primary schools.

The PE teacher must inspect all equipment and apparatus in the gymnasium to see that it is in good order. Arrangements should be made for the equipment to be regularly tested and a note kept of the dates of inspection. It is recommended that such apparatus be tested at least three times a year by a competent person so that defects due to wear and tear may be discovered and made good. It would be desirable for LEAs to arrange an annual inspection by firms who supply pieces of apparatus. However, the teacher should ensure that all apparatus, both fixed and portable, is of a suitable design and construction. Portable apparatus should also be stored when not in use.

Teachers should, under no circumstances, permit apparatus which is obviously damaged to be used in lessons. It is important in the context of the discharge of the duty of care that steps are taken to prevent foreseeable accidents.

Special care has to be exercised in the use of apparatus. This was underlined in the case of *Kershaw v Hampshire County Council* (1982) (unreported) concerning the use of a trampette in a class of 12 year-old girls.

A girl was injured when she was vaulting and somersaulting over a box. She ran and bounced on the trampette but went too high and too fast and fell. The judge found that it was known, or should have been generally known to responsible organisers in the field, that the use of a trampette was somewhat more dangerous than the use of the normal springboard and the use of the trampette did have a greater tendency to lead to an accident.

The plaintiff had already participated in the exercise successfully and there were two girls acting as catchers. Unfortunately, the teacher left the gymnasium to go to the office just prior to the girl's accident and there was therefore no supervising adult.

The judge found that the teacher should have been present to provide the necessary support and supervision throughout this particular exercise and that if the teacher had to leave the pupils, either to go to another group or to leave the gymnasium, she should have stopped the activity until her return.

The availability of space and equipment must always be carefully considered, and in those urban schools where, for instance, hard surface playgrounds are the only open places available for PE or games, the children may very well have to forgo some of the best group exercises and games.

In halls and gymnasia, it should be seen that there are no low windows of ordinary plate glass if the pupils are to be allowed full range for their PE activities. In the case of *Ralph v London County Council* (1947) III JP 548 a pupil was taking part in a game of "touch" being played in the school assembly hall under the supervision of a teacher. One side of the hall consisted of glass partitions with doors in them, the glass partitions being three feet from the ground. During the game the pupil, whilst being chased by another boy, unwittingly put his hand through one of the glass partitions. The judge held that the reasonable and prudent father would have contemplated that such an accident might have happened and that the boy was accordingly entitled to damages. The decision was later upheld in the Court of Appeal.

Guidelines issued by the Health Education Authority (*The Use of Sunscreens in Schools: A Good Practice Guide*, 1999) warn against excessive exposure to sun. It has been reported (The Times, 5 July 1995) that, although it did not admit liability, an LEA has paid compensation to the parents of a pupil who suffered severe sunburn after engaging in sports activities outside for five hours without protection. The Health Education Authority recommends that schools should draw up policies, in collaboration with parents and governors, to increase knowledge, influence behaviour and create an appropriate environment for pupils to stay safe in the sun. Such a policy would provide for sun awareness to be included in appropriate areas of the curriculum and for staff to follow protection procedures. Special precautions are advised for sports days, when the use of sun screen should be permitted, and for children with fair skins. The guidelines also suggest school dress and areas of shade in school grounds as issues to be considered.

PLAYING FIELDS AND EQUIPMENT

The **Education (School Premises) Regulations 1999** require a minimum playing fields area in any school where there are pupils aged eight or over (pupil referral units are excluded).

Playing fields must be:
- suitable for the playing of team games
- laid out for that purpose
- capable of sustaining the playing of team sports for at least seven hours per week during term time.

Schools may have other provisions for sport/physical education other than grass playing fields. For example:
(a) a hard porous surface, sufficiently large to accommodate team games (this will count as twice its actual area)
(b) synthetic surfaces suitable for some team sports
(c) other areas that could count for a reduction of grass area and facilities for:
(d) regular instruction in swimming (school or off site)
(e) indoor instruction in team games (school or off site)
(f) outdoor instruction in team games (off site).

The minimum total playing field areas in m^2 for schools other than special schools are given in the table below.

Total number of pupils aged eight or over	Schools with pupils under 11: Minimum total area in m²	Other schools
100 or less	2,500	5,000
101 to 200	5,000	10,000
201 to 300	10,000	15,000
301 to 400	15,000	20,000
401 to 500	20,000	25,000
501 to 600	25,000	30,000
601 to 750	30,000	35,000
751 to 900	35,000	40,000
901 to 1,050	40,000	45,000
1,051 to 1,200	45,000	50,000
1,201 to 1,350	50,000	55,000
1,351 to 1,500	55,000	60,000
1,501 to 1,650	60,000	65,000
1,651 to 1,800	65,000	70,000
1,801 to 1,950	70,000	75,000

For schools with over 1950 pupils, the minimum total area should be equal to the aggregate of 70,000 or 75,000m² plus 5000m² for each complete 150 by which the number of pupils exceeds 1801.

A Sporting Future for All contains a section headed *Sport in the Community*. Within this section the report recognises that "playing fields in particular provide a vital recreational resource for schools and local communities". The report also recognises the problem of the loss of too many valuable playing fields and that inevitably this has affected grassroots sport. At present local authorities are required to consult Sport England for all planning applications involving sports pitches. The **Town and Country Planning (Playing Fields) (England) Direction 1998** requires local planning authorities to refer to DETR minutes of planning applications on playing fields which they are minded to approve, but where Sport England are against. The Direction was a joint initiative between the Department for Education and Employment (DfEE), the Department for Culture, Media and Sport (DCMS) and the Department of the Environment, Transport and the Regions (DETR). It is intended to act as an additional safeguard for the protection of playing fields from sale.

Section 77 of the **School Standards and Framework Act 1998** empowers the Secretary of State to protect school playing fields in England from disposal or change of use. These powers are explained in DfEE Circular 3/99 *The Protection of School Playing Fields*. The **Education**

(School Premises) Regulations 1999 creates school premises standards including for playing fields under the heading: *Team Game Playing Fields.*

Paragraphs 94–104 of Circular 3/99 contain comprehensive details of definition, quality, minimum area, shared team playing surfaces, all weather surfaces, balance of grassed and all weather surfaces, location, etc. Of equal significance *Outdoor Play Equipment* specifies: "equipment used in school including outdoor/day equipment is not covered by the Regulations."

Yet the equipment used in schools for outdoor as well as indoor activity is equally important as the playing fields themselves and of vital significance when considering health and safety requirements.

Chapter 2 contained a reference to the out-of-court settlement for a rugby playing injury caused by a concrete obstruction (it was in fact a concrete base of a dividing barrier between the rugby deadball line behind the goalposts and an adjoining tennis court). The other examples which may be regarded as samples in Chapter 2 are of a vaulting horse (*Gibbs*) and a polished floor (*Gillmore*) and are illustrative of the dangers existing within the use of recreational equipment.

A recent DTI report (*22nd Annual Homes Survey*) identified more than 824,000 people were treated at casualty for sports related injury in 1998.

"...sporting equipment was involved in many accidents and was blamed for many injuries. Slipping gym mats were the cause of 11,210 accidents and there were 6000 collisions with goal posts."

Collapsible football crossbars have caused fatalities and occupy the attention of the FA. FIFA, the National Playing Fields Association and the British Standards Institute (BS EN 748).

The England and Wales Cricket Board has recommended, after taking legal advice, that those participating in pupil cricket matches should wear protective helmets. Malfunctioning equipment can create an indemnity claims for defective products.

The attention of Heads is drawn to the booklet *Safety in Swimming Pools* published jointly by the Health and Safety Commission and the Sports Council early in 1988. Swimming pools are covered by the **Health and Safety at Work, etc Act 1974** which requires employers, eg LEAs or governors, to ensure as far as is reasonably practicable, the health and safety of employees and others who use the workplace and its facilities. Although not prescriptive the guidance offered by *Safety in Swimming Pools* is likely to be taken into account by inspectors of the Health and Safety Executive (HSE) and enforcing authorities in deciding what is "reasonably practicable" for a pool operator to do.

CHAPTER 6

CLUB CO-OPERATION AND CO-ORDINATION

A Sporting Future for All recognised at paragraph 8.30 on page 41:

"Professional sports clubs can play a key role in the development of sport. There are many interesting examples in rugby league, rugby union, cricket and football which demonstrate their valuable contribution. Professional clubs are a significant community resource and elite competitors can prove to be a great source of motivation for young people. Many already provide extensive community programmes including out-of-school learning opportunities for young people. Other sports related businesses such as clothing and equipment manufacturers offer support to school and community initiatives."

The following paragraph 8.31 continues:

"Our new programme Playing for Success is part of our drive to expand study support and out of school hours provision utilising professional soccer clubs as focal points for young people. The centres offer programmes focused on improving literacy, numeracy and IT skills mainly for young people who are disaffected or are likely to become so. Forty clubs are committed to opening centres and 29 are already open. This programme provides an excellent example the way that local education authorities, schools and major sports clubs can work together with DfEE support to provide new and motivating opportunities for young people to learn in a different environment."

The integration of the role of clubs to that already discussed for schools and parents is vital to the full enjoyment of sport and recreation and to the development of potential elite competitors. The **Local Government Finance Act 1988** provides rate relief by local authorities when premises are linked to charitable purposes. Clubs which structure their affairs in order to provide opportunity for coaching, teaching and training can therefore accrue financial benefit. Club affairs may be arranged beneficially for VAT purposes as has been confirmed in the case of a bowls club in Somerset which successfully separated outdoor and indoor sections.

Charitable status as an element of physical education under the House of Lords decision in the FA Youth Trust case of 1980. The case concerned whether the Charity Commissioners registration (in 1972) of an FA Youth Trust Deed was valid. The key to the registration as a charity being that physical education is legally regarded as educational. Charitable status also exists under the **Recreational Charities Act 1958** as an element within social welfare, particularly following a further House of Lords decision in 1992 from Scotland inspired by the North Berwick Sports Centre.

One of the methods endorsed by a former Chief Charities Commissioner for activating these advantages was for clubs which operate youth or school sectors to hive them off as separate entities to take advantage of fiscal benefits which will follow.

This in turn allows for claims for rate relief by clubs activating these advantages under sections 47(1) and (2) of the **Local Government Finance Act 1988**. Clubs which link with schools to provide out of hours physical education assistance would thereby qualify for these criteria with appropriate and adequate financial and administrative guidance endorsed and approved by the Charities Commission.

This contributes to community based physical education in accordance with the *A Sporting Future for All* strategy. Law does not differentiate between levels or categories of activities or disciplines. Teachers, coaches and parents are all bound by the duty of care to minimise risk. In addition the same requirements for the safety of premises and equipment apply.

CHAPTER 7

MEDICAL ISSUES

A key issue of concern has been the lack of overall guidance and medical supervision in the provision of school sports. It is significant to note that the DoH was not involved in the *A Sporting Future for All* strategy.

There is no clear government structure that places sports medicine in schools. The Medical Officers for Schools Association (MOSA) has a membership of approximately 500 but this association is only concerned with the independent education sector. British Association for Sport and Exercise Sciences has about 1000 members but is not overtly concerned with school sports.

Physical education for schools is therefore dependent upon general medical services without specialist physical education services specialities. It is desirable that arrangements are made to try to liaise with local speciality sports and health centres. Medical sources also crucial for alerting and identifying potential child and drug abuses as well as potentially serious injury.

The MOSA handbook (concerned as stated above with the independent sector) identifies that:

"...as a result of the burgeoning interest in exercise and the large amounts of money often involved in professional sport, sports medicine is now a speciality in its own right. School doctors will often find a nearby consultant colleague who professes an interest in sports injuries. Physiotherapists too often specialise in treating competitors. Usually run through private practice they often attach themselves to a local leisure or sports complex. Links with such are worth fostering. It is possible that they may be persuaded to provide regular clinics at the schools to the benefit of both."

Schools should therefore examine links to their advantage and seek so far as is practicable links with the sources of sports medicine. Medical services for school sports are likely to be called upon to deal with:

- first aid and immediate management of injury; even if not present at time of injury, he/she may be called upon to advise members of staff who will be there
- basic orthopaedics, chiefly the recognition and management of sprains fractures and soft tissue injuries
- demands and risks of sports practised at school, so that can advise pupils.

In addition the prevention of injury is of key concern. As stated earlier in this book it is important that participants are aware of the safety requirements of an activity. It is vital to spell out any inherent dangers. In some pursuits (eg climbing, caving and scuba) safety is a major component of the sport which must be learnt by the newcomer.

Players who are unfit are more likely to be injured. A large part of any sport is learning how to avoid the risk of injury. A skilled horse rider is less likely to fall or be thrown than a novice: a rugby team with adequate preseason training is less likely to have someone injured in a scrum. All participants should be taught the importance of warming up and warming down with appropriate exercises.

Doctors and coaches should co-operate and insist on the use of appropriate equipment. For some sports this is mandatory:

Riding	hard hat
Rugby	mouthguard/gumshield, shin pads
Hockey	mouthguard, shinpads
Cycling	helmet
Squash	goggles

Recently the England and Wales Cricket Board has attracted unfavourable press comment from its insistence that junior participant should wear helmets while batting or fielding close to the batsman. Discussions in the media have suggested that coaches have a choice in implementing this directive though evidence would suggest they do not. It is difficult to see how the coach could excuse failing to introduce the safety measure recommended by the sports governing body.

Furthermore should participants wish not to wear protective equipment the coach or supervisor must consider the extent to which the participant has a full appreciation of the risks. Particularly where peer pressure may further compromise the judgement of the pupil. Additionally schools may face a dilemma should parental wishes excuse the child from wearing a helmet. The prudent school will side with increased protection for the participant.

SUPERVISION, REFEREEING AND SELECTION OF TEAMS

The rules of a game and manner in which they are enforced will influence injury toll. Laws of RFU for example have been amended with aim of reducing the risk of injury in the set scrum and the ruck, and the introduction of different rules for younger players has helped to protect from harm. Clearly the governing body of each sport may needs to be consulted for any amended rules for juniors where these are not clear.

It should also be noted that adolescents of the same age can vary widely in size and strength. There is a danger of teams or individuals being inappropriately matched if selected by age rather than size, skill or strength.

MANAGEMENT OF SPORTS INJURIES

It is not in the scope of this text to address medical issues or competence. It is interesting to note that a distinguished American orthopaedic surgeon with a special interest in knee injuries insisted that personal observation of the mechanism of injury was vital for accurate diagnosis. (For that reason he felt obliged to be present at all the fixtures of his favourite team to whom he was honorary specialist.)

Many independent schools insist on a doctor being present at First XV rugby matches though except in rare cases of spine injury or life threatening collapse (and assuming that in those cases resuscitation equipment and neck immobilizers are available) it is unlikely that physical presence will add anything vital to management. Indeed injuries are as or more likely on junior pitches. However as mentioned previously a prudent school may examine partnerships with external agencies to provide better medical services.

Immediate early management of injuries is key. The acronyms RICE and ERICA are often used to suggest procedures for the immediate treatment of specific soft tissue injuries.

R	— rest
I	— ice
C	— compression
E	— elevation

E	— elevation
R	— rest
I	— ice
C	— compression
A	— aspirin

Such readily obtainable information cannot be a substitute for medical advice. It is always the case that if pain is severe or persists then a doctor should be seen.

A British Sports Council survey in 1991, *National Study of the Epidemiology of Exercise*, into sports related injury illness concluded: in summary of the injuries and exercise main report:

"Six million new sports injuries require treatment each year. Accident and Emergency departs are well equipped to deal with the more serious injuries, but family doctors may be less familiar with the management of sports injuries. To help reduce costs and improve effectiveness the way in which sports injuries are managed should be reviewed. NHS Sports Injury clinics may be needed to fill the gaps."

Six years later a leading article in the *British Journal of Sports Medicine* from Dr Robin Knill-Jones (June 1997, pages 95-6) recorded:

"Sports related injuries for a significant part of the workload of the National Health Service. Patients with acute injuries account for between 3.9% and 7.1% of total attendance at casualty departments, and a higher proportion of attendance — 28% by children. An unknown proportion of these injuries go on to become chronic or recurrent problems which later involve orthopaedic clinics or GPs. Clearly there is an unmet need for expert advice and treatment for which NHS resources appear unavailable."

Thus it may be argued that sports medicine (and its ethical criteria) with its uniquely complex and rarely recognised general and specialist multi-disciplinary requirements, which are rarely understood within both sport and society and medicine generally, stands apart from other medical and paramedical areas.

CHAPTER 8

HEALTH AND SAFETY

The **Health and Safety at Work, etc Act 1974** (HSWA) has been applied to prosecutions in school labs. However the author is unaware of prosecutions regarding physical education; however in relation to equipment safety and standards it does exist as a weapon in legal armoury to protect pupils and may yet be invoked for PE and Sport — particularly with stronger attention from the inspectorate.

The **Management of Health and Safety at Work Regulations 1992** (MHSWR)were introduced to implement European Community health and safety legislation and in particular the Framework Directive which sets out requirements for a health and safety regime based on prevention of accidents and injuries. The 1992 Regulations, subsequently replaced by 1999 Regulations of the same name, extended the obligation to carry out risk assessments first introduced by the **Control of Substances Hazardous to Health Regulations** (COSHH)to all hazards at the workplace.

> "Formally to identify the hazards present in any undertaking and to estimate the extent of risks involved taking into account those precautions which are already in place, to the health and safety of employees and others who may be affected in order to identify measures needed to comply with relevant health and safety legislation."

Risk assessments are an essential part of a health and safety management system and the Regulations require employers to introduce measures for planning, organising, controlling, monitoring and reviewing their safety management. One of the benefits of a sound health and safety management system is that teachers and other staff can be confident that they can rely on well planned health and safety arrangements when they are carrying out the their own responsibilities.

The Health and Safety Commission offers advice on health and safety management in *Managing Health and Safety in Schools* (1995). It stresses the importance of schools having a written health and safety policy which sets out their commitment to health and safety arrangements. To make a health and safety policy work there needs to be a positive health and safety culture. There has to be a pro-active, not a reactive, approach to health and safety.

In schools this means carefully considering what could harm pupils, then identifying and putting in place precautions to reduce or prevent that harm. It must be recognised that everyone has responsibility for health and safety. Individuals have different responsibilities and each individual's specific responsibilities and limitations should be clearly understood.

The MHSWR require employers with more than 5 employees to make written risk assessments for employees and for non-employees such as pupils. The Regulations do not stipulate how a risk assessment should be set out except that it should be carried out by a "competent person" with sufficient training, knowledge and experience to be able to assess the risks properly. Additional assistance may be necessary for the risk assessment. This comes from external consultants but internal expertise should be sought in the first instance. For schools this may be available through health and safety advisors or safety representatives or other colleagues.

Pupils can be usefully involved, in day to day risk assessments at the start of lessons and during lessons depending on their age and ability. Involving pupils in this way makes them aware of potential harm and of the importance of being able to take as much responsibility as possible for their own safety. In December 1999 the QCA, with assistance from the Health and Safety Executive, produced a new general health and safety teaching requirement for science, design technology, information and communication technology, art and design and physical education. It requires that when working with tools, equipment and materials, in practical activities and in different environments, including those that are unfamiliar, pupils should be taught:

- about hazards, risks and risk control
- steps to control the risk to themselves and others
- to use information to assess the immediate and cumulative risks
- to manage the environment to ensure the health and safety of themselves and others

- to explain the steps they take to control risks.

In physical education health and safety education can be integrated into schemes of work by way of topics such as safety rules, safe use of equipment, safe handling of equipment and apparatus, particularly safe lifting techniques and knowing and applying accepted techniques for particular activities.

Health and safety training should also be included in the personal, social and health education (PSHE) programme. This should include understanding risk and how to assess potential danger.

Identifying hazards and assessing the related risks are at the heart of a risk assessment. A hazard is anything that could cause harm and a risk is the chance that someone may be harmed by the hazard. If there are no hazards there are no risks. Assessing the extent of risk involves identifying the individuals who might be affected and the consequence for them: ie quantifying the hazard. Not all hazards create a risk and some risks are so small that they can properly be ignored. It is not the function of a risk assessment to try to eliminate all conceivable risks to anybody. Pupils should not be placed in situations where they are exposed to an unacceptable level of risk and safety must always be the important consideration.

Once hazards and risks have been identified the next stage is to take action. In PE and Sport this may sometimes be quite simple, for example, adjusting equipment that is at the wrong height or taking broken or damaged equipment out of use until it is repaired. In other situations the risk may need to be addressed in a more fundamental way by changing the teaching process or how the activity is carried out. Alternatively the activity may need to be substituted by a safer activity. The risk assessment may show that pupils are not made aware of safety procedures or that more attention needs to be given to discipline, control or supervision.

Risk assessments have to be "suitable and sufficient". This is set against the back-drop of the general obligation in the HSWA that employers must do what is "reasonably practicable" to ensure the health and safety and welfare of employees and non-employees at the workplace. The duty holder must weigh up the severity of the risk against the cost in terms of time, effort and money needed to control that risk.

The application of health and safety issues in the sporting arena may, just as with the principal academic aspects of the schooling process be all embracing. However, the core issues largely reduce to a logical appraisal or assessment procedure. Provided this process has been properly evidenced and implemented, the potentially onerous duties may be lessened considerably.

The health and safety requirements on head teachers or governors as regards sports, and, for the purposes of this chapter, other activities apart from day to day classroom teaching, are exactly the same as those affecting core teaching activities. At the risk of repetition these are set out below. However, the very variety of sporting activity, ranges of site and of sporting providers (eg from games teachers to other suppliers of sports coaching and instruction either on or off the school premises) means that the health and safety issues arising from them may be rather more complicated, and as a result require specific consideration.

In brief, every different activity and venue of the pupil's environment needs to be considered from a health and safety viewpoint; all risks assessed as to their severity and possible frequency and, where possible and reasonably practicable, steps taken to minimise or reduce that risk. In addition to pupils, this process should also be undertaken for employees and any other person permitted to be on the premises or involved in the activity sponsored or managed by the school, eg parents, helpers or other visitors.

Failure to comply with health and safety requirements can result in criminal prosecution, and a possible personal summons against the governors or head teachers. Fines may be unlimited. Although a breach of health and safety legislation does not, in itself, generally give rise to civil liability, (eg claims for compensation under the tort of negligence) the very fact of a prosecution will nevertheless represent good capital in a civil claimant's action. A failure of the requirements of health and safety legislation may also found a good case for a civil action for negligence as it probably indicates that supervision generally fell below that to be expected of those *in loco parentis*.

Also, publication of action taken by the Health & Safety Executive, be it at worst a summons and possible conviction, or prohibition or improvement notices, two lesser but nevertheless significant steps that can be taken by the HSE, may all generate extremely unfavourable publicity for the school.

LEAs also retain the right to inspect premises and, if remedial steps are not implemented, carry out work themselves and counter charge the school.

The purpose of this chapter is to set out the framework and practical implementation of the Health and Safety legislation. This inevitably covers points which will already have been implemented in the schools other spheres. It will then consider its application to the sports and other related activities.

DUTIES

Under the HSWA, employers have the general duty to their employees to ensure "so far as is reasonably practicable" their health safety and welfare. This duty is further explained with reference to the need for employers to provide "such information instruction, training and supervision as is necessary to ensure, so far as is reasonably practicable the health, safety and welfare at work" of all employees.

Employers must conduct their undertakings so as to ensure "so far as is reasonable practicable" that persons not in their "employment who may be affected thereby are not thereby exposed to risks to their health or safety."

Furthermore the duties include the need for persons who are not the employer but who have:

"to any extent, control of premises...to take such measures as it is reasonable for a person in his position to take to ensure, so far as is reasonably practicable, at the premises, all means of access thereto or egress there from available for use of persons using the premises, and any plant or substance in the premises or, as the case may be, provided for use there, is or are safe and without risks to health."

Points Arising

1. The duties set out above are imposed on employers. With LEA controlled schools the employer is the LEA. However responsibility for, and adherence to health and safety standards together with their implementation are still requirements of the head teacher or governors.
2. The governing body is usually the employer in all other schools.
3. As well as duties on employers towards employees, the duty also extends to pupils, and school visitors who may be parents or other persons permitted to be on the school premises, or involved in the school activity.
4. Premises include school grounds.
5. The scope of the duty extends to an "undertaking", which will include school organised activities both on and off the site.

6. "Undertaking" could include the quality of training of staff or supervision of pupils during an activity set up or managed by the school.
7. The standard for the implementation of the safety measures of reasonable practicability implies a balancing test of the risk of injury between, on the one hand, the severity and frequency of the risk and, on the other, the time, cost and trouble involved in either removing the potential risk altogether or minimising it to an acceptable level.

SAFETY POLICY

In addition to the principal duties set out above, s.2 (3) of the HSWA requires employers to both prepare a written statement of the general policy with respect to the health and safety at work of employees and to revise the policy "as often as may be appropriate". The policy must include the organisation and arrangements in force for carrying out the policy. In addition the employer must "bring the statement and any revision of it to the notice of all of his employees."

One of the benefits of a sound health and safety management system is that teachers and other staff can be confident that they can rely on well planned health and safety arrangements when they are carrying out their own responsibilities. The Health and Safety Commission offers advice on health and safety management in *Managing Health and Safety in Schools* (1995). It stresses the importance of schools having a written health and safety policy which sets out their commitment to health and safety arrangements. To make a health and safety policy work there needs to be a positive health and safety culture.

It is beyond the purpose of this chapter to detail all of the areas to be considered in the preparation of a policy statement. In LEA controlled schools, the LEA will have a general policy statement which may require adoption and amendment by the specific school. Schools which are not LEA controlled will have to prepare their own statement. LEA advisers however can often provide invaluable assistance in this area, together with the preparation of risk assessments which are discussed below.

Policy Statement

The purpose of the health and safety statement is to publicise a commitment in the organisation to the aims of the health and safety legislation; and how specific aspects of that commitment are to be delegated, reviewed and disseminated.

The policy statement will be a document in which the employer (or person delegated by the employer) will provide undertakings to provide a safe place for staff and pupils, including equipment and systems which are safe; it will also undertake to provide adequate supervision, training and instruction for the tasks and activities that the pupils and staff may be called upon to perform. There will almost certainly be a reference to the provision of adequate safety and protective clothing and welfare facilities.

The policy document may then set out the organisation and responsibilities of the staff to implement this policy statement. The responsibility will often rest principally with the head teacher. The duties of the head may include:

- the delegated responsibly for ensuring the health and safety of pupils staff and others on the school premises or taking part in school activities
- the adoption of safe working practices; arranging systems of risk assessment; identifying training needs
- ensuring that any defects in equipment or premises are rectified insofar as is practicable
- responsibility for the collation of accident and incident information and, where necessary, the investigation of these areas
- the promotion of health and safety.

Similar delegation may also be made to other "supervisory" members of staff.

In addition to the above, the policy statement may also refer to the health and safety issues relating to hirers, contractors or other persons involved in the school activities. One would also expect references to emergency plans, training, medical and first aid issues, and also an undertaking in relation to special needs pupils.

Sports and other non-educational activities may not necessarily require specific mention within the health and safety policy statement. However it is suggested that factors which may determine whether sport merits a specific reference in the statement are:

- the type and size of school
- the amount and variety of sport played
- the variety and location of the site or sites where sport is played
- the variety and incidence of other activities sponsored by the school.

This might mean that a member or members of staff could be given specific health and safety delegation for the following areas:

- sport activities in the school

- sports premises and equipment
- off-site sport or other outdoor activities of the school.

As with specific delegation to the head, any such "sports" delegation should set out that member of staff's responsibilities; the frequency of any required checks or assessments of equipment and premises; how the outcome of such checks should be recorded; and, where necessary, a record kept of any maintenance, replacement or training initiated. It is suggested that any such section could be easily worked into the existing safety policy statement. There are a number of reference materials which could be of assistance, not just from controlling LEAs.

It is important that the policy statement is not only workable but also properly implemented and regularly reviewed. It is also important that it is properly brought to the attention of all employees.

RISK ASSESSMENT

The MHSWR 1999 have replaced the previous **Management of Health and Safety at Work Regulations 1992** and have set out the requirement for compulsory risk assessments. It also places other requirements on employers.

The Regulations require the employer to undertake risk assessments of the undertaking's activities to act on issues generated by this exercise, and to inform his workforce and review those measures from a continuing Health and Safety viewpoint. The Regulations also go further, touching on an employer's first aid requirements, adequate training for employees; training and induction of new or temporary employees. Specific consideration is also required of an employer of young employees.

Regulation 3(1) of MHSWR require all employers to undertake a "suitable and sufficient" assessment of the risks to which employees are exposed in the course of their work. In addition the employer must assess the risks to persons not in employment but who are affected by the conduct of the undertaking. In addition when identifying control measures the employer must "comply with the requirements and prohibitions imposed...by or under the relevant statutory provisions."

Those statutory provisions include the duties set out under the HSWA above in relation to the requirement on an employer to make his undertaking to employees or others as safe as is reasonably practicable.

An assessment needs to be reviewed if there is reason to suspect that it is no longer valid or if there has been a significant change in the matters which it covers.

An employer employing more than five employees must record the significant findings of the assessment and any group of his employees identified by it as being especially at risk.

Any preventive or protective measures implemented as a result of the risk assessment exercise need to be carried out in accordance with the principles set out at Schedule 1 of the Regulations. These range from avoiding risks altogether to replacing dangerous by non-dangerous or less dangerous measures; evaluating risks which cannot be avoided; giving appropriate instructions to employees.

Regulation 5 requires the employer to make and give effect to the planning, monitoring, and review of the "preventive and protective measures". Regulation 5(2) requires that a record be kept of the conducted reviews and, at least by implication, the steps actually taken to implement those measures.

The Regulations include requirements that the employer inform his employees about the risk assessments and the resultant preventive and protective measures (regulation 10).

Regulation 12 also sets out a framework for the health and safety of employees from an outside undertaking at a "host" employers. On the one hand, they require the host employer to provide comprehensible information on the risks to the guest employee's health and safety. In addition, there is a requirement on an employer to ensure that the employer of the guest employee is also provided with sufficient information to comply with the requirements for emergency evacuation procedures.

Procedure

The risk assessment procedure will be undertaken by the governing body or delegated to specific members of staff in relation to certain areas such as classroom safety or other safety around premises and activities. The risk assessment needs to be "suitable and sufficient", ie that all appreciable hazards have been considered as to their potential incidence and severity of outcomes for both employees and others on (or off) the premises, and consideration then given to the risk elimination or reduction.

Any potential high frequency, high severity, risk noted from the risk assessment will require minimising or removal altogether if the employer is to provide the safe system of work to employees, or fulfil its duty of care to non-employees as required under the HSWA as set out above.

The preparation of a risk assessment requires five distinct phases, namely:

1. Consideration of the hazards.
2. Consideration of the likely people who may be affected by the hazards detected in 1, above.
3. Assessment of the likelihood of injury occurring and consideration of the hazards and the persons likely to be affected both in terms of frequency of accident and the potential severity; and consider whether any steps could be reasonably taken to remove or reduce the risk.
4. Recording the first three steps above.
5. A review of whether any amendments have been made to 1, 2 and 3 above and, perhaps more importantly, whether any decisions or recommendations made following the earlier risk assessment have been implemented.

HSE information leaflets (*Five Steps To Risk Assessment*) are a useful guide, as is Croner's *Croner's School Health and Safety: Records and Procedures* package.

The circumstances for the provision of sport (and other activities) at each establishment will lead to the decision whether a complete risk assessment should be undertaken for each activity or for each facility with, in effect, a sub-assessment for each of the range of activities which occur in each facility.

Consideration of the event or activity before it takes place should cover the foreseeable hazards. Factors which one might need to consider before embarking on a list of the hazards themselves may be:

- any special education or equipment needs, or medical consideration
- any hazards in relation to the size, age or group of participants in the event
- changing facilities
- movement or travel to the activity area
- fire regulations
- first aid
- the activity itself
- equipment
- staffing supervision and adequacy of staff: pupil ratios
- emergency action and procedures.

It is suggested that in relation to the preparation of risk assessments for sporting activities, the assessor will need to consider three general areas:

1. Premises.
2. Equipment.
3. Coaching, training and supervision.

There is clearly an overlap between premises and equipment in some instances.

It is difficult to provide specific advice when the circumstances for each risk assessment will be unique. However examples of issues to consider for a "premises" (a gymnasium) and an "equipment" assessment (rugby) are set out below. Neither is intended to be exhaustive.

Pupils can be usefully involved in day to day risk assessments at the start of lessons and during lessons depending on their age and ability. Involving pupils in this way makes them aware of potential harm and of the importance of being able to take as much responsibility as possible for their own safety. As mentioned earlier there is a general requirement to teach health and safety to pupils when working with tools, equipment and materials, in practical activities and in different environments, including those that are unfamiliar (for science, design technology, information and communications technology, art and design and physical education). Pupils should learn:

- about hazards, risks and risk control
- to recognise hazards, assess consequent risk and take steps to control the risk to themselves and others
- to use information to assess the immediate and cumulative risks
- to manage the environment to ensure the health and safety of themselves and others
- to explain the steps they take to control risks.

In physical education, health and safety education can be integrated into schemes of work by ways of topics such as safety rules, safe use of equipment, safe handling of equipment and apparatus, particularly safe lifting techniques and knowing and applying accepted techniques for particular activities.

Health and safety training should also be included in the personal, social and health education (PSHE) programme. This should include understanding risk and how to assess potential danger.

Example 1 — Premises: Gymnasium

Flooring Loose boards, uneven, cracked or splintered flooring requires attention. Synthetic floors which are prone to breakdown should also be reviewed. Floors should not be polished to a slippery finish and dust kept to a minimum.

Walls These should be smooth to avoid grazing or other friction injuries. If there are sharp edges, especially once again where body contact is likely to take place, protection should be provided. Items such as light switches should be positioned, where possible, above working height or otherwise recessed.

Doors These should have some sort of restraint or fastener. Glass doors should be carefully considered to minimise the risks of breakage and injury (see below).

Glazing and lighting Glass, wherever necessary should be reinforced and resistant to fracture. Cracked panes should be replaced as a matter of urgency. Artificial lighting should be secured in protective cages and strip lighting maintained to minimise flickering. Consideration should be given to reducing dazzle caused by sunlight in early spring or late autumn.

Heating and ventilation Heating components must be designed to remove any danger to any of pupils being affected by burns, fumes or other hazards; consideration ought to be given to the location of exposed pipework.

Showers and changing rooms Consideration should be given to the adequacy and maintenance of flooring, especially tiles which can crack. Shower mixer valves should be positioned out of the reach of children to prevent scalding. Pegs should be positioned at an appropriate height and should be of a pattern to minimise bending or distortion.

Example 2 — Equipment: Rugby Union/League

Boots These should fit properly with adequate ankle support.

Studs These should conform to the appropriate British Standard and should be examined regularly for wear. Badly worn studs should be replaced.

Shin guards These should be made of light material and secured in position. They should also be worn by all players.

Shoulder padding These should consist only of light, protective, padding and conform to the recommendation and requirements of the International Rugby Board.

Mouth guards These should be recommended as a valuable means of protection.

Goal posts and corner flags The bases of the uprights for the goal posts should be padded to avoid any direct contact, so should any other obstacles close to the touch line. Corner flags should be flexible and smooth with rounded ends.

COACHING, TRAINING AND SUPERVISION

Adequate supervision is perhaps the most crucial element in a risk assessment of any sporting activity. Its control and management are probably the most important issues as they also combine an appreciation of the suitability of premises and equipment.

The supervision of the activity needs to be undertaken by appropriately experienced and qualified (or accredited) staff, who should be able to run this activity with the given age and amount of the pupils involved. Issues which touch on this area are:
- the experience and qualifications of the supervisor
- the ability to control and teach the group of pupils
- the necessity for any other personnel to supervise or assist the activity
- the qualifications and experience of any other assistants.

It is suggested that the experience and qualifications of the principal teacher should include the ability to deal with any medical emergency and first aid in addition to the ability to teach or coach in the activity itself.

OFF-SITE ACTIVITIES

The very range and variety of off-site activities which schools may provide for their pupils either regularly or as single events throws into sharper relief the need for suitable and sufficient risk assessments (see also Chapter 4). They still form part of the school's undertaking and therefore require assessments. This exercise is likely to be conducted hand in hand with the detailed planning and organisation for the activity.

It is outside the terms of reference for this chapter to consider all of the issues which need to be considered when planning for an out-of-school activity. However, there appear to be certain recurring aspects which will need specific consideration by both the teacher organising the activity and, in turn, the head teacher in authorising the activity to proceed, and these are touched on below:

Activity Provider

Is the activity to be organised by the school or by another organisation? If by the school, it will require a full detailed risk assessment, almost certainly with a preparatory visit so that all hazards can be assessed and appropriate arrangements made.

If, on the other hand, the activity is to be provided by an outside organisation, it is imperative that the school ensure that the providing organisation has complied with all health and safety legislation such as the provision of a policy statement, and risk assessments. In effect, the school must ensure that the providing organisation is competent and adequate for the proposed activity.

In relation to certain outward bound activities, the providing organisation must be licensed, in accordance with the **Activity Centres (Young Persons' Safety) Act 1995** and **Adventure Activities Licensing Regulations 1996**. Activities which require a licence are caving, climbing, trekking, and water sports.

Residential Activities

If the activity is to take place off-site overnight, the risk assessment and planning exercise will need to consider specifically the adequacy of the proposed accommodation in terms of layout, fire precautions, recreational facilities.

Equipment

Consideration will need to be given as to whether the school need supply any further additional equipment and, in the event that the activity provider is to supply equipment, its adequacy and sufficiency.

Supervision and training

Whether the school is going to arrange the activity itself, or use the services of an activity provider, it is essential that there are adequate and suitably experienced or briefed teachers and other staff or helpers. In addition, it is essential that pupils involved in the activity receive sufficient briefing and explanation prior to the commencement of the activity.

Depending on the age of the pupils involved in the activity, there should probably be a minimum of one teacher for every 10 pupils.

The use for instance of an off-site swimming pool will require consideration of the level of supervision and first aid/emergency procedures at the pool with those of the school.

Transport

The use of hired coaches, private cars, transport in a school mini-bus or some other means of transport will raise a number of additional areas for consideration such as parental consent, adequacy and competence of other parent/helper drivers, and the safety of minibus or hired-in transport.

Parental Consent/Medical/First aid

The adequacy of first aid equipment for any school activity is clearly one of the aspects which must be considered on any risk assessment either at the school or off site. In addition, the supervision for the activity must also include the experience of the staff to be able to provide adequate first aid in the event of an emergency.

Apart from the ordinary misfortunes of cuts and fractures which could be anticipated from the assessment of the activity itself, certain pupils may also have known medical complaints which may give rise to an emergency situation requiring the administration of medicines or drugs. This is something which will need to be addressed not only in relation to the school's existing medicine policy, but also in relation to whether the parents are prepared to consent to such treatment being administered by the teachers as necessary in their discretion whilst involved in the school activity. Parental consent will be required anyway for the school visit and in particular, consent to any emergency dental, medical or surgical treatment, including anaesthetic or blood transfusion considered necessary by the medical authorities.

A model form for parental consent can be found in the Department for Education and Employment's *Good Practice Guide: Health and Safety of Pupils on Educational Visits 1998*. There are two other DfEE good practice guides that cover first aid and medicines in schools. These are *Guidance On First Aid For Schools - A Good Practice Guide* (1998) and *Supporting Pupils with Medical Needs* (1996).

Emergency and Contingent Procedures

Part of the risk assessment process will require either the implementation or reviewing of emergency and contingent procedures. This should cover not only the eventuality of problems arising during the course of the off-site activity, but also in the event of early return to school for, eg bad weather. Contact numbers for parents and head teachers should be readily available.

ON-SITE ACTIVITIES

Hired in Sport or Activity Providers

Two issues arise in consideration of provision of sports or other activity lessons on the school premises by an outside party. Initially, the school needs to ensure that the outside provider is made aware of the school's health and safety policy statement, (as is the case with building contractors working on site) and to comply with any site safety requirements. In addition, the activity undertaken by the sports provider may necessitate a specific risk assessment to be carried out by the school to incorporate that activity.

In addition, the school needs to enquire that the sports provider is competent to provide the services supplied and in this respect will need to check the provider's health and safety policy statement (if appropriate) and risk assessment. Assurances will be required as to the safety of any equipment supplied or proposals for use on the school site.

Extra Curricular Activities

Attention should also be drawn to the health and safety requirements in the event of sports or other activities being granted to pupils and parents on the premises, but not specifically organised by the school, eg the use of swimming pools out of term time, weekends, etc. This will require specific consideration in terms of risk assessment and training. For instance visitors may only be permitted to use the swimming pool on certain conditions, such as:

- a minimum of two adults on site at any time, one of whom is lifeguard trained
- numbers of supervisors to children using the pool
- general training and awareness of all users of the pool
- knowledge of emergency procedures and contact numbers.

VETTING

Another issue which this situation may generate relates to the vetting of persons in contact with young persons. The same consideration also arises in relation to the provision of helpers on outward bound or off-site activities, or activities using an off-site provider. The school or group leader needs to ensure the suitability of volunteers or other providers of sports activities, eg drivers, helpers, etc.

The **Education (Teachers) (Amendment) Regulations 1998** prevents people barred by the Secretary of State from being directly employed by any school or further education college by banning them from working either as a volunteer, or working in a business that is contracted to provide services to schools or further education institutions.

The identity of those banned by the Secretary of State can be checked by a request either through the LEA, or, in the case of independent schools and further education institutions, via the Department for Education and Employment. Such checks should be made in all appropriate cases.

REPORTING SCHOOL ACCIDENTS

Again, at the risk of repetition of procedures which will already be in force at the school, it is appropriate to draw attention to the requirements of the **Reporting of Injuries, Diseases and Dangerous Occurrences Regulations 1995** (RIDDOR Regulations). The primary responsibility is for accidents which result in death or major injury, or accidents which prevent the injured person from continuing his or her normal work for more than three days, to be reported, initially, by telephone as soon as possible, and thereafter within 10 days by completion of form 2508 which should be returned to the Health and Safety Executive. The primary duty is in relation to accidents involving employees.

The definition of accidents now includes an act of non-consensual physical violence which would include violence done to a teacher during the course of his or her employment.

Major injuries are also defined in the Regulations. It does not include fracture to the fingers, thumbs or toes.

Accidents involving pupils or other visitors to the school premises need also to be reported if the person involved is either killed or taken to hospital and the accident arises out of or in connection with work. The latter would be an accident arising out of or in connection with work if it is attributable to, for instance, the supervision of a field trip, or the condition of premises (eg a cut caused by glass or other debris on a playing field). In short, accidents involving anyone in the sporting or extra curricular activity field may require reporting to the Health and Safety Executive, and no doubt also to the LEA.

There is also a reporting requirement in the Regulation for dangerous occurrences.

CHAPTER 9

INSURANCE

The purpose of insurance is to help the school protect its property and meet its legal obligations without having recourse to the funds needed to deliver education. Even where the LEA arranges insurance, the school itself should be familiar with the small print on the policies for the following reasons:

- those arranging cover may not be familiar with all the school's activities and so may overlook the significance of particular policy provisions (or lack of them)
- many legal obligations may rest with the governing body of the school, whoever arranges cover
- the school may need to inform staff, pupils, parents and others of limitations in policies to ensure that the school's activities remain within the policy wording — or to allow parents to arrange separate cover
- prompt payment of a claim will depend on the school's ability to show that it has complied with the terms of the policy
- the school also needs to know when to require external organisations to have cover, for example those hiring the school's facilities or external course providers.

CATEGORIES OF INSURANCE

Most insurance contracts are contracts of indemnity, that is they pay out a sum of money when the insured has proved a pecuniary loss resulting from an insured event. Some insurance contracts, for example personal accident cover, do not require financial loss to be proved, but merely require the happening of an insured event such as loss of limb. The main types of insurance cover are:

1. First party insurance — this provides cover against loss and damage to property owned by the school, for example sports equipment or buildings, either due to specific perils such as fire or flood or, less frequently, "all risks". It also includes personal accident cover.
2. Third party insurance — this provides cover for the school's legal liability to third parties, for example if the school's negligence results in injury by failing to referee a rugby match in accordance with rules or inadequately supervising a swimming lesson.

Some insurance policies, for example motor policies, cover both types.

ADMINISTRATION OF COVER

Independent sector schools will be accustomed to making their own insurance arrangements either direct with insurers or through a broker who may be able to offer economies of scale by arranging block policies.

Maintained schools may rely wholly on their LEA or may make some of their insurance arrangements through a broker or direct with insurers. Although maintained schools may now call for the whole of their delegated budget, in practice when it comes to insurance many will continue to take advantage of the knowledge and purchasing power of their LEA.

Insurance provisions vary considerably between LEAs. A small number self-insure. Others offer a menu of different types of cover or a standard package. Some types of cover may not be available from your LEA and may need to be arranged privately. Maintained schools opting out of LEA block policies may be required to allow their LEA to inspect the policies and ensure that LEA interest is noted on the policies. It is in the school's own interests to comply with these requirements to avoid a dispute with the LEA in the event of a claim.

Types of Cover

The main types of cover that affect schools are:

- property and contents — buildings including those connected with sport, such as pools, pavilions; sports equipment owned by the school, its staff and pupils; sports equipment owned by visitors such as visiting school teams
- motor — school minibuses; staff vehicles; visitors' vehicles; hired coaches, etc
- employer's liability
- public liability

- professional indemnity
- personal accident
- governing body's liability
- business interruption
- key person cover
- permanent health insurance
- travel insurance
- legal expenses insurance.

Importance of Full Disclosure

It is the school's obligation to disclose all relevant information when asking an insurer to give cover for the first time, and there is the same obligation on renewal. If the information is inaccurate or incomplete it could result in the school having no cover at all. The person who looks after insurance for the school is responsible for making all the necessary enquiries so that full and accurate answers may be given to the questions on the proposal form and any other questions insurers may ask.

Questions to Ask

1. Is the policy still in force and when is renewal due?
2. Who will arrange for renewal?
3. Who will be responsible for ensuring that full disclosure has been given and that the policy has been renewed?
4. For whom is the cover needed, eg governors, staff, temporary staff, pupils, volunteers, visitors?
5. Is the level of cover adequate?
6. Are there any gaps in the cover, eg geographical constraints, cover off the school premises, property not belonging to the school, pupils on work experience, volunteers on self-help schemes?
7. Are there any exclusions?
8. Does the insurer impose any special conditions; if so, are they being complied with?
9. Can the school prove to insurers that any special conditions are being complied with?
10. Do staff/pupils/parents and other relevant parties know about any exclusions and limitations?
11. Are there any special requirements about reporting claims?
12. Do the relevant people know about them?

13. Has anything material to the risk changed since cover was first arranged?
14. Is there an excess (sometimes called a "deductible") and if so has it been budgeted for?
15. If there is an excess, is the amount payable for each claim or each occurrence, eg one occurrence, such as a locker room fire, could give rise to numerous claims.

Details of the school's insurance arrangements should be provided in the school prospectus.

Understanding the Policy

Insurance policies are not always easy documents to follow and disputes about policy wordings are common. If you do not understand a wording take advice from your LEA insurance department or the provider of the insurance when the policy is taken out — do not wait until you have to submit a claim. If possible, get a written response from the insurer, but in any event make a full written note of any enquiry at the time it is made, including details of the person to whom you spoke about it and when, and the response received.

The key documents are:

• the proposal form
• the schedule — this usually shows the amount of cover and any excesses
• the policy wording — this is usually the document containing the terms and conditions which govern your contract with insurers; it should be read in conjunction with the schedule and any endorsements or extensions (see below)
• endorsements — these include special terms and conditions of the policy which are not included in the general policy wording; sometimes there is a standard list of endorsements and only certain endorsements will apply to your particular policy
• extensions — these are extensions to the cover, for example, using the school sports field for a charity fete
• certificate of insurance (some policies).

When reading an insurance policy, you need to consider all parts of the policy including the schedule, policy wording, endorsements and extensions and how the different sections inter-relate. For example, a clause explaining the cover needs to be read with the exclusions section. The policy wording may also impose important conditions about reporting claims.

Many policies have definitions sections which ascribe specific meanings to certain words and phrases. The Courts have defined others. In the absence of a definition either by the insurer or the Courts, words are usually interpreted as having their ordinary and natural meaning. Where there is ambiguity, the words will usually be interpreted against the party who drafted the wording. If in doubt about the meaning of a policy wording, do not make assumptions — seek advice.

Buildings and Contents

The following questions should be addressed:

1. Is the level of cover adequate — does it cover the current cost of rebuilding; it is important to ensure that the level of cover is kept under review to ensure that there would not be a shortfall in the event of a claim?
2. What is covered — are there any gaps; eg children's own equipment, staff's own equipment, items over a specific value, equipment belonging to visiting teams or other visitors?
3. Where is it covered — on school premises, in the main buildings or in a sports pavilion; at other schools, when visiting external sports facilities; where used overseas?
4. What is the limit per claim, per occurrence and in total for the policy year in question?
5. Are staff/parents/pupils aware of any limitations on cover or on the sum per claim — is cover "new for old" or on a different basis; is cover for certain items limited, eg clothing or jewellery when left in changing rooms; what is the total amount per claim; are certain activities excluded; will any behaviour by the school, staff or pupil result in cover being refused; what if the claim arises from the pupil's own carelessness?
6. Are there any special requirements such as fire or security precautions imposed by insurers?
7. Are staff, pupils and others aware of those special requirements — is the school complying with them?
8. Can you demonstrate to insurers that the school has complied with any special requirements?
9. If the claim proceedure for loss or damage to pupils' contents to be part of call in any claim, or a "contingent" cover, ie only to be claimed against if there is no household policy arranged by then parents.

Motor

Motor insurance is required by law so provided the school is satisfied that any parental or other visiting vehicle is taxed, the school can reasonably assume that the vehicle is insured unless of course there is evidence to the contrary.

For incidents involving motor vehicles which occur on the public highway, there are statutory arrangements in any event even if the driver of the vehicle is not insured.

If vehicles are used off the public highway, the compulsory insurance requirements may not apply and the school is advised to check what arrangements are in place. For the school's own vehicles, all the general points above about insurance apply. In addition:

- ensure that all relevant information regarding the driver's/the school's insurance history is disclosed on renewal; keep a written record of any claims for ease of reference and to ensure that important information is not omitted
- ensure that only those covered by the policy drive the vehicle; ensure that insured reserve drivers are available for all outings
- ensure that seat belt requirements are observed by staff and pupils even on the shortest journeys
- ensure that passenger doors are locked
- do not pick up hitch-hikers
- keep valuables out of sight when leaving the vehicle
- ensure that the vehicle is properly maintained; routine checks on tyres (including spares), seat belts, etc must be carried out regularly; ensure all those responsible for these checks understand their responsibilities and adhere to them without exception
- ensure that all drivers understand what to do in the event of an accident; drivers and passengers should avoid making admissions of liability or statements which could be interpreted as admissions of fault; such statements might prejudice their school's/LEA's/insurer's position in the event of a third party claim
- ensure that teaching and other staff using their own vehicles in relation to school activities have notified their insurers and have appropriate cover; insurance policies are interpreted very strictly in relation to "social, domestic and pleasure driving" and with "business" driving — even if the journey was undertaken in an emergency — insurers may still refuse to pay; it may be appropriate to issue guidelines to staff that their own vehicles should not be used in any circumstances

- ensure that where teachers are acting as agents of the school, for example in relation to district or county sports activities, cover is provided
- compulsory motor insurance is not required to cover employees suffering death or injury in a road traffic accident in the course of their employment provided that it is covered under the employer's liability policy; in law, who is an employee and what is in the course of their employment is not straightforward; you need to be sure that your motor/employer's liability cover has no gaps; if in doubt, check with your LEA, insurer or broker.

Employer's Liability

Employer's liability insurance enables employers to meet their legal liabilities up to the policy limit for claims arising from injury to the school's employees. For example: if a teacher trips over a protruding goal post socket negligently left in place and uncovered by ground staff at the end of the football season; if a teacher suffers a back injury due to having to move heavy apparatus without the appropriate assistance, training or equipment; if a teacher suffers from stress related illness induced by his or her working circumstances.

LEAs are exempt from the **Employer's Liability (Compulsory Insurance) Act 1969**, the Act which makes employer's liability compulsory for most other employers. However, DfEE Circular 2/94: *Local Management of Schools* makes it clear that LEAs will either act as insurers or arrange for insurance to cover the potential liabilities of employers, so in practice LEA maintained schools should have employer's liability cover.

Schools which are not maintained by their LEA are not exempt under the 1969 Act and therefore have a statutory obligation to have employer's liability cover in accordance with the Act.

Even where the Act does not apply, the school should not have less than the statutory minimum cover required under the Act. The statutory minimum level of cover is set out in the **Employer's Liability (Compulsory Insurance) Regulations 1998**. The minimum cover is currently £5m in the aggregate for claims arising from any one occurrence.

The Regulations require this cover to be in force without any element of self-funding, that is without any excess or deductible being paid by the employer. The Regulations prohibit insurers from including certain policy terms and conditions which would otherwise allow them to avoid cover. The school needs to consider:

- whether the statutory minimum level of cover is adequate and seek a higher level of cover if necessary — words such as "each and every claim" and "per occurrence" need to be read carefully (see *Public Liability* cover below); bear in mind that in relation death or injury to employees certain motor accidents may be covered by your employer's liability cover rather than your motor policy (see *Motor* above); if serious injuries were caused to several teaching staff in an accident when travelling in the school minibus in the course of their employment, £5m per occurrence may not be adequate if the school was held to be negligent (perhaps by being vicariously liable for the driver's inattention or excessive speed); the school may have to make up the shortfall
- whether all those classes of people the school requires to be covered are actually covered — if necessary, ensure that you have alternative cover; eg agency or self-employed supply teachers or volunteers or students on teaching practice
- ensure that where teachers are acting as agents of the school, for example in relation to district or county sports activities, cover is provided.

Public Liability

Public liability cover protects the school against the cost of claims brought by members of the public in relation to the school's activities. For example: if a passer by is injured by a cricket ball (and the school is culpable in some way); if a light fitting in a gymnasium falls and injures a visiting basketball player; if a pupil is injured due to wearing insufficient protection during a rugby match; if pupils on an excursion cause damage to a member of the public's property.

The "public" potentially covers: pupils; parents and other visitors to the school such as other schools' sports teams; visiting contractors; volunteers involved in self-help schemes — for example, painting the changing rooms; other volunteers; other service visitors such as delivery people; members of the public with whom pupils come into contact on excursions and outside the school grounds; members of the public in the vicinity of the school premises; rescuers in an accident; in certain circumstances, trespassers.

Make sure the school is aware of any limitations on the cover. For example, cover for motorised water sports is usually excluded.

Make sure insurers are aware of any unusual circumstances which may give rise to a risk, eg funding activities, evening classes or summer schools, use of school playing field for firework displays and bonfires, use of swimming pool for private lessons or in the school holidays, use of facilities by local sports teams or other groups.

Where external groups use school premises, for example a local charity using the school field for a car boot sale, the school must ensure that the organisers have their own public liability insurance or an extension to the school's policy bought and paid for by the school to cover the event under their own cover and included under the hire charge. Parent/teacher associations may be regarded as an independent body so you should not assume that the school's insurance covers their activities.

Where pupils are entrusted to external organisations, ensure that their public liability cover is adequate and that their staff have the appropriate qualifications (see Chapter 8, Health and Safety).

Where pupils are attending other organisations on work experience, ensure that you know whether they are being covered by your own or the employer's insurance.

Ensure that where teachers are acting as agents of the school, for example in relation to district or county sports activities, cover is provided. Some LEAs include this cover; others do not.

Make sure that levels of cover are adequate, paying particular attention to whether the limits are per claim or per occurrence. If for example the gymnasium ceiling collapsed and several children sustained brain or other very serious injuries, £5m per occurrence would not be sufficient on the basis of sums currently being awarded by the court. The shortfall would have to be met by the school/LEA.

Professional Indemnity

Professional indemnity insurance provides cover for the school/LEA in relation to claims arising out of their staff's failure to show the necessary skill and care in the exercise of their professional duties. It is likely to become increasingly important following the recent House of Lords ruling in the area of learning difficulties.

Personal Accident

Personal Accident provides cover for accidental injuries. It frequently has a tariff based on specific types of injury such as loss of an eye or limb. Some policies include related cover such as a hospitalisation benefit. Personal accident policies for pupils may be offered by the school to the parents or guardians. Policies in the independent sector may reimburse parents for school fees if their child is unable to attend and could be used to fund private tuition.

Personal accident policies pay out on the occurrence of a particular injury or loss and unlike employer's liability or public liability, it is the injury or loss of use rather than legal liability to a third party which triggers a payment under the policy. For example:

- if a pupil suffers spinal injury while using the school's trampoline, despite adequate maintenance, instruction and supervision by the school, a personal accident policy would (depending on the injuries covered and the policy wording) pay out, even though a public liability policy would not
- if a pupil loses his sight in one eye due to piercing by a twig on a cross country run the pupil would receive the sum agreed for loss of sight in one eye (subject to the policy wording) irrespective of the school's liability.

Points to consider are:

- check that the level of cover is adequate for the purpose
- be aware of any policy exclusions such as motorised water sports and do not permit pupils to participate in these activities
- make sure that parents and guardians, staff, volunteers and those in charge are aware of any exclusions
- wilful misconduct may in some circumstances enable the insurer to refuse to pay a claim
- if in doubt about whether certain circumstances should be notified to insurers check with them before the activities are carried out
- remind helpers and other relevant individuals that they may wish to arrange personal accident cover as the school's liability cover would only respond in the event of the school's negligence, it would not respond if there had simply been an accident that was no one's (or the victim's) fault.

Business Interruption

In the independent sector where school fees might be lost in the event of an insured peril such as fire, cover may be available to replace lost income. The school's broker should be able to assist with ascertaining an appropriate level of cover.

Key Person Cover

Key person cover provides financial protection for the school in the event of the incapacity of key staff. Such policies usually pay a lump sum to the insured (ie the school) upon the illness of nominated persons which would help to cover the costs of providing a temporary or permanent replacement and other expenses. When weighing up the costs/benefits of the cover, the school needs to consider in particular:

- the position regarding pre-existing medical conditions; eg if a member of staff has a pre-existing injury at the time the cover was taken out, the policy may not pay out if a deterioration in the condition forces the teacher to have surgery followed by a prolonged convalescence
- the type of illness/injury covered under the policy; cover may be limited to serious illnesses such as heart disease or cancer but exclude more common conditions.

Permanent Health Insurance

Permanent health cover pays an agreed percentage of the salary of a member of staff who is unable to work due to illness or injury. This sum is paid to the employee, helping the school to avoid the need to pay both the sick person and their replacement.

If the person is unable to return to work, the policy will usually pay an agreed percentage of their salary for a pre-agreed period, depending on their capacity to carry out other work: eg a PE teacher with a severe knee injury may not be able to return to full-time PE teaching, but may be capable of carrying out lower paid work.

As with key person insurance, it is important to consider the small print in relation to the cover that is being offered carefully in order to weigh up the costs/benefit to the school. In particular, it will be important to consider:

- the position regarding pre-existing illness or injury
- the range of circumstances in which payment would (and would not) be made; cover usually only commences after an initial period of absence, during which the teacher would have to be paid by the school/LEA in accordance with their contract of employment, the policy may cover less common conditions and exclude those which are more likely to occur.

Cover for the Governing Body's Liability

Provided governors act honestly and reasonably and within their powers when exercising their functions, any liability will fall on the governing body rather than the governors individually.

The governing body as a legal entity needs insurance cover to protect the governing body in the event of its own negligence in performing its duties. Some LEAs provide this cover for LEA funded schools out of central funds. Others allow individual governing bodies to "buy in" to block policies. If the governing body does not have cover from the LEA, it will need to provide its own.

Governors may also wish to arrange cover for individual governors, although this may prove expensive. It should not be necessary provided the governors conduct themselves appropriately, but it is clearly a matter for the governors whether they require this protection.

Admission and exclusion appeal committees are not committees of the governing body. LEAs are required by the **School Standards and Framework Act 1998** to indemnify members of these committees against any legal costs and expenses they may reasonably incur in the exercise of their functions as members of these committees.

Cover which provides similar protection for the school's governing body and members of that body is available for schools in the independent sector.

Travel Insurance

When arranging cover for school travel, consider the following points:
- seek specific advice from your LEA insurance department, insurer or broker about any specific requirements for health cover/insurance in the country to which you are travelling
- disclose details of any particularly hazardous activities in which staff/pupils will be participating to insurers and ensure that cover is provided
- make sure the travel cover includes adequate levels of cover for healthcare and the costs associated with accident or illness abroad such as additional hotel expenses, transport by air ambulance, etc
- make sure that those travelling bring adequate supplies of any medication in their hand luggage (provided it is safe to do so)
- make sure those travelling and parents are aware of any limitations on cover such as cover for cash, limits for any one item such as cameras

or jewellery; make copies of the insurance schedule available to parents as early as possible in the booking process

- check any limits on cover for delayed baggage or additional transport arrangements and make pupils and their parents aware of these limits
- make sure if possible that the school is covered in the event of having to delay or cancel the trip, for example for staff illness
- where there are limitations in the policy consider imposing identical limitations on pupils travelling, for example in relation to amounts of cash or value of items
- ensure pupils are security conscious; take common-sense precautions such as closing windows when leaving accommodation and ensuring that valuables are not left unattended in changing rooms, etc
- if you are travelling with the school's own vehicle you will need to ensure that you have complied with any legal requirements for that country; motoring organisations such as the RAC and AA can usually advise — again, consult your LEA, insurer or broker about specific legal insurance requirements in the country concerned.
- ensure that the policy provides for legal assistance in relation to the recovery of claims; if sports equipment is being hired, ensure that your policy provides cover for damage to or loss of hire equipment, or that this is included in the hire agreement.

Legal Expenses Insurance

Legal expenses insurance proves cover against the cost of the school's own legal fees and any legal costs awarded against the school in the event of certain types of legal dispute. Cover is usually only provided where legal expenses insurers consider the school has reasonable prospects of winning or successfully defending the dispute.

You will need to consider the limit offered by the policy carefully as legal costs can escalate rapidly and also be aware of whether the limit is per claim or for claims arising from one originating cause. The "Woolf" civil litigation reforms introduced in recent years means that costs are often front-loaded because courts encourage parties to prepare their case in full early in the proceedings.

Certain types of dispute may be excluded and the policy needs to be studied carefully to ensure that the school is actually getting the cover it requires. If in doubt, talk to your insurer, broker or LEA.

The policy will usually not cover a dispute of which the school is aware at the time the policy was taken out, unless the dispute has been disclosed to insurers and they confirm cover will be provided.

IN THE EVENT OF A CLAIM

Under many liability policies, insurers have the right to bring legal proceedings or defend legal proceedings in the name of the school. Early notification gives insurers the opportunity to exercise their rights from the outset. All claims and potential claims should be reported to insurers at the earliest opportunity. Check the notification requirements in the policy. If there is any delay the insurers may be entitled to refuse to give cover.

Where there has been an injury in a sports match or lesson, the potential for a claim may be obvious. In others, it may be less obvious but the circumstances should nevertheless be reported to insurers. Some policy wordings may require the school to notify circumstances which may give rise to a claim, for example: where there has been an injury, but no suggestion that the person injured will sue the school; the injured person will have three years from the date of the injury to bring a claim.

Where there has been an accident or injury, the following will need to be considered:

- if an injury is involved, make sure the accident book/report form is completed in accordance with the school's reporting procedure; bear in mind when completing the entry that it may be disclosable to any party considering suing the school — even before legal proceeding have been issued
- do not express views on the cause of the accident at the scene of it
- **Reporting of Injuries, Diseases and Dangerous Occurrences Regulation 1995)** requirements should also be dealt with (see Chapter 8, Health and Safety); death or major injury must be reported to the Health and Safety Executive immediately
- if appropriate, for example in a road accident, make a sketch of the scene, showing approximate distances and any road signs, markings; date the sketch
- if possible, take photographs of the scene of the accident
- record the full names and addresses of any witnesses
- take short factual statements from witnesses as soon as possible after the accident; these statements should not express any opinion as to the cause of the accident but should merely document what they saw, heard and did; the statements should include the full name and address of the witness; the witnesses should sign and date the statements.

- make sure that original sketches and statements are copied and kept in a safe place
- keep any apparatus/equipment involved in the accident in a safe place, labelled with the date of the accident and name of the person injured; if litigation follows, expert witnesses may need to inspect it; if the accident was caused by a defect in the equipment it may be necessary to involve the supplier or manufacturer in any subsequent litigation; if the apparatus needs to be dismantled or removed following the accident ensure that insurers have the opportunity to send an expert to examine it first
- remember when anything is documented about the claim, for example in internal memoranda, correspondence and minutes of meetings, these documents may become disclosable if litigation ensues
- any opinions on liability or admissions of fault should be avoided where possible, although if there is Health and Safety issue, the school must deal with it in accordance with the school's established procedure; it may be prudent to alert your insurer to the fact you are obliged to implement this procedure.
- if the claim arises from criminal activity, for example arson or theft, a crime reference number should be obtained from the police for the claim form.

Ensuring that Claims are Paid

An insurance policy is a contract between the insurer and the insured. As with any other contract, there are terms and conditions which have to be adhered to, for example: activities such as motorised water sports may be excluded, conditions may be imposed relating to claims notification, certain behaviour such as consumption of drugs or alcohol may invalidate cover.

The courts are always reluctant to interfere in a commercial contract entered into by two organisations, both of whom have access to legal and business advice. Insurers therefore can and do avoid paying claims where insureds have not abided by the policy terms and insurers' rights have been prejudiced.

Prompt payment by insurers without a dispute can reduce the risk of legal proceedings being issued against the school and may therefore minimise the time individuals at the school will need to spend dealing with it. This can also help to minimise adverse publicity.

To minimise the risk of an insurer rejecting your claim:

- check the small print of any policy upon which you rely and comply with it; keep records to show you have complied
- know what is excluded; avoid excluded activities or arrange alternative cover
- make sure staff, volunteers and others are aware of any exclusions
- advise insurers immediately in writing if circumstances change
- keep an insurance file so that you do not forget to disclose previous claims to insurers on renewal.
- it is better to pay a slightly higher premium than find insurers will not pay when a claim is made
- ensure that you have disclosed any fact which might affect the insurer's decision to offer/continue cover or fix the premium when arranging cover; previous claims, cancellations of cover and refusals of cover are all relevant; failure to disclose such information could enable insurers to avoid paying the claim
- notify claims or circumstances which might give rise to a claim as soon as possible
- follow the school's own guidelines and official guidelines (for example HSE and DfEE) in relation to health and safety procedures and exercise good practice at all times
- remember that claims may affect your school's future premiums; some LEAs relate premiums to the school's level of claims and others are considering doing so; having insurance is therefore no substitute for exercising care.

Further Information and Disputes

Talk to your local LEA insurance department, broker or legal advisers.

CONCLUSION

This chapter has highlighted some of the aspects of insurance that schools need to consider in order to ensure that they have adequate protection. Insurance arrangements will inevitably vary from one school/LEA to the next. Policies also vary enormously when it comes to the small print. It is therefore imperative that in relation to insurance matter you take individual advice.

Insurance advisors should co-ordinate with clients. A lack of adequate communication can lead to adverse results. One example occurred through inadequate co-ordination preventing sufficient preparation to avoid a judgement for liability against a governing body.

Premiums are inevitably tailored to the risk involved. Factual co-ordination at every level in prevention and response to injuries will be crucial for every level of activity.

CHAPTER 10

FUNDING

Traditionally school sports have been funded through the normal system of departmental allowances. Transport to matches and refreshments might have been paid for by contributions from team members or from funds provided by the PTA or from parental contributions to the School Fund.

Local shops and businesses have often been willing to sponsor shirts for school teams. But there are now many additional sources of funding. Some of them make a considerable difference to what schools are able to provide for their own students and, in some cases, for students from the wider community.

THE NATIONAL LOTTERY

The National Lottery is a major source of funding from which schools can benefit. Sport was one of the specified good causes to benefit from the Lottery when it was set up in 1995. The stated Lottery fund strategy is to provide equal opportunity of access to sport and to help those with talent to develop into sports stars of the future. For every Lottery ticket sold 3.8p goes to sport — over four years £1 billion has been invested in capital sports projects across England and a further £100 million has gone into revenue schemes.

Most lottery-funded programmes give special emphasis to schemes intended to benefit those living in areas of socio-economic disadvantage; the aim is to improve access to sport for groups traditionally under-represented, such as girls, members of ethnic minorities and those with special disabilities.

Schools, along with sports clubs, local authorities and national governing bodies of sports can apply for Lottery grants. The money available is distributed by Sport England, Sport Scotland and the Sports Council for Wales. The grants available and the rules vary between the different parts of the United Kingdom. Full details are available from the relevant web sites:

- www.sportengland.org.uk
- www.sportscotland.org.uk
- www.sports-council-wales.co.uk
- www.sportni.org

New Opportunities Fund

A source of government funding for which schools can apply is the NOF. There are grants of up to £200,000 available for the provision of out-of-school-hours learning programmes. These proposals can include sport but are likely to cover a much wider range of activities.

School Community Sports Initiative

In England schools are able to apply for grants to build new sports facilities or to upgrade existing ones through the School Community Sports Initiative. Up to 80% of the capital cost is available if the scheme meets specified criteria: for example the facility must be available for community use for 40 hours per week and must lead to a significant increase in participation or a measurable improvement in sporting standards. A similar scheme operates in Wales, while in Scotland the Sports Facilities programme will fund projects which include the provision of reception areas, changing accommodation, lockers, showers and fixed or portable equipment.

Awards for All

Another set of grants which schools can access includes Awards for All. Originally known as Millennium Awards for All this community small-projects programme has been extended and is due to run until March 2002. It aims to provide sums of £500 to £5000 to small local groups such as youth groups or sports clubs. However a school linked with a local club that uses its facilities could apply for a grant.

TOP Programmes

An excellent set of resources to support the PE national curriculum in primary schools is available through the TOP Sport and TOP Play programmes run by local authorities. Both programmes are organised by the Youth Sports Trust in conjunction with the three national sports councils. TOP Sport is intended for 7-11 year olds and introduces children to nine different sports:
- basketball
- cricket
- football
- hockey
- netball
- rugby
- squash
- table tennis
- tennis.

The programme provides sports/activity specific resource cards, equipment and training and support for teachers. TOP Play is similar but intended for 4-9 year olds. It introduces children to essential sporting skills such as running and jumping, throwing and catching, striking and kicking, travelling with a ball and receiving a ball. The equipment provided is child-friendly and multi-coloured and includes mini-racquets, bats and balls, bean bags, quoits and markers.

School Sports Co-ordinators Programme

Primary schools and secondary schools can benefit from another lottery-funded government initiative, the School Sports Co-ordinators programme, the first phase of which was launched in September 2000 with the establishment of 33 schemes in England. This is a multi-agency initiative that will link schools, local communities, local sports facilities, clubs and sports' governing bodies to deliver a range of new opportunities.

The expected model for the scheme is usually likely to involve a Partnership Development Manager working with four or five secondary schools. Within each of these secondary schools an experienced teacher will act as the School Sports Co-ordinator, working with up to five primary or special schools for two or three days per week. In each of the associated primary or special schools an experienced teacher will ensure that the agreed programmes are planned and delivered. This teacher will be released for one or two days per month to work on the initiative.

100% funding is provided for the scheme in the first year but 10% partnership funding is required in year two and 20% in year three.

SPECIALIST SPORTS COLLEGES

The government is making a major financial input into school sports in England through its Specialist Schools Programme. By the beginning of 2001 some 83 schools had been designated as Specialist Sports Colleges and further applications are invited, although preference will be given to schools in some LEAs over others to ensure a good geographical coverage.

The amount of money available to the specialist schools is considerable. There are two elements: a figure for a capital project; and a per capita figure for recurrent expenditure.

For the capital project schools, including those designated from September 2000, had to raise £100,000 in private sponsorship — matched by a DfEE grant of £100,000. In the most recent round of applications the sponsorship figure was reduced to £50,000 which everyone agreed was more easily achievable.

The *per capita* grant during the current financial year is £120 (plus an allowance for inflation) for schools with up to 1000 on roll and a further allowance for any pupils over 1200. This grant, available for up to four years in the first instance and possibly renewable for a further four years, is for additional staffing, specialist coaching, equipment, staff training and other costs: all of which are geared to the achievement of targets set out in a specialist school's development plans. These plans must set out clearly how the school will expand provision and raise standards not only in school sports but also in the wider community.

Many specialist sports colleges are putting resources directly into their partner primary schools as well as providing increased coaching opportunities open to all young people in the locality.

SPORTSMATCH-BUSINESS SPONSORSHIP

Sportsmatch is the government's grass roots sports sponsorship initiative scheme, and similar schemes exist for England, Scotland and Wales. The aim is to encourage business to invest in sport by matching money obtained in sponsorship pound for pound. Schools as well as other not-for-profit groups can apply.

Matching awards are available between £1000 (£500 for a school) and £50,000. The sponsorship can be in cash or kind (in the form of sporting equipment). Grants can be for capital (up to £5000) or revenue projects. The latter include coaching, competition, equipment, and hire of facilities.

Further details are available on the website: www.sportsmatch.co.uk

SPORTS' GOVERNING BODIES

Schools may have links with the governing bodies of particular sports, many of which have County Development Officers. Schools have been able to access funds for a variety of initiatives and some aspiring specialist schools have been able to get sponsorship to support their applications.

The Lawn Tennis Association (LTA) is particularly generous in providing grants and loans. Grants of up to £50,000 are available to up-grade tennis courts where community access is provided. Schools which apply also have to agree to establish a sinking fund to pay for long term maintenance. The amount varies according to the type of surface: for example, for porous macadam £1000 (plus an amount for inflation) per court per year must be put into the sinking fund. This will cover costs of resurfacing, cleaning and repainting.

Further information is available on the LTA website:
www.LTA.org.uk

LOCAL AUTHORITIES

As part of the National Curriculum children should be able to swim by the end of Key Stage 2 and so LEAs normally fund swimming for primary schools. Some may also fund swimming for secondary schools. The costs may be included in the LMS formula allocation or there may be direct funding.

Local Authorities, both County and Borough, may also fund a variety of other sports initiatives open to schools and details will be available from the relevant leisure, recreation or sport department.

CHARITABLE TRUST

Schools have applied to local or national charitable trusts for help in the past and no doubt will continue to do so. Individual students can often benefit from grants for sports equipment, specialist coaching courses, school sports tours and other necessary travel.

Reference books such as *The Directory of Grant Making Trusts*, published by the Charities Aid Foundation, list the names of the major national trusts and the purposes for which they will make grants. However schools will probably find that they and their students have most success with local trusts and it is a good idea to build up a positive relationship with them, perhaps by inviting in representatives to meet staff and students.

Help with out-of-school-hours learning activities is available from Education Extra, a charitable trust which offers funding up to £2500 to support any club which a school wants to set up out of normal school hours, including a club for a particular sport. 50% of grants are up to £250, 40% £250–£1000 and 10% £1000–£2500.

Education Extra is supported by a wide range of companies. Further details are available on www.educationextra.org.uk

CASE STUDY

An interesting example of funds being brought together from several sources was reported in the Eastern Daily Press (07.02.01). A Cricket Development Officer to be based at a King Edward Vll School in King's Lynn, a specialist sports college, has been appointed as a result of a partnership between the school, the West Norfolk Borough Council, the Norfolk Cricket Board and HSBC Bank.

Sports College money was available for a part-time appointment; the NCB and the borough council arranged sponsorship from HSBC which was Sportmatched. This enabled a full-time appointment to be made. Among many other activities, Kwik Cricket will be developed in local primary schools.

CHAPTER 11

GOVERNMENT

There are thirteen separated departments actively concerned with sport and physical education but these are not co-ordinated. Government involvement with sport has existed since even the Norman Conquest times (protecting archery by banning football). Similar involvement can be traced to **Physical Education and Training Act 1937** in anticipation of World War II.

Since then the crowd stadium disasters at Ibrox (1971), Bradford (1985) and Hillsborough (1989) have created judicial enquiries and safety legislation. Alongside these development, public health legislation and current education act legislation have provided for physical education in legislation. Section 508, **Education Act 1996** provided for functions in respect of facilities for recreation and social and physical training, s.149 provided for dual use facilities. Furthermore the **Local Government Finance Act 1988** in ss.47 and 48 provided for rate relief at varying levels for recreation and sporting organisations.

The thirteeen bodies involved in sports are as follows:

1. Department for Culture Media and Sport (DCMS) — a Minister for Sport exists
2. Department for Education and Employment (DfEE) — education
3. Department of Health (DoH) — health and sports medicine
4. Department of Environment Transport and the Regions (DETR) — playing fields
5. Department of Trade and Industry (DTI) — accidents
6. Home Office — drug related legislation
7. Ministry of Agriculture Fisheries and Food (MAFF) — sport and recreation on agricultural land

8   Lord Chancellor's Department — Law Commission and consultation papers and judicial enquiries

9   Attorney-Generals Office — papers and judicial inquiries, Crown Prosecution Service and foul play, criminal violence and misconduct

10   Treasury — Inland Revenue and VAT legislation for sport and recreation

11   Welsh Assembly — issues affecting region

12   Scottish Parliament — issues affecting region

13   Northern Ireland Assembly — issues affecting region

All sports have governing body concerned with promotion, coaching etc. Most have section relating to sport in schools and physical education: eg helmets for cricket and insurance for rugby.

The governing sporting bodies position in relation to physical education is equally elusive and fragmentary as the government departments listed above. Consider the 113 different VAT exempt non profit making activities listed in Chapter 2 and the resulting multiplicity of governing bodies with administrative constitution, framework and organisation. In some cases these are staffed by volunteer officers.

The extent to which individual bodies will or will not be concerned with physical education must depend upon its financial resources, its will to activate interest in physical education and the capacity to recruit appropriately skilled PE practitioners/liaison.

Separate and apart from governing body structures are the self autonomous schools sports associations which can be affiliated to or in competition or contention with a governing sporting body. The English Schools Football Association and the English Schools Cricket Association reflect this position, usually administered by school teachers.

Yet separate from and transcending the adult volunteers and the dedicated others are the physical education teachers. Nearly ten years ago in 1991 a House of Commons departmental inquiry into sports in schools produced a Professional Association of Teachers response that primary schools were neglected in the area of competent physical education. The then Government's ceiling on teaching hours discouraged traditional out of schools coaching — the position was seen to be almost irredeemable.

The issue of integration is therefore essential to *A Sporting Future for All* with a view to deciding what action to take and where, when and how the appropriate services are to be deployed.

CHAPTER 12

THE FUTURE

As a result of the success in the Olympic games and the para-Olympic Games a great surge of enthusiasm and active interest in further participation for all physical education in the United Kingdom is inevitable.

On a weekly basis there are media reports of the problems of a lack of adequate physical exercise being undertaken by children and adults. Recent research directly links levels of physical activity to academic success.

Physical education is and will continue to be a headline issue and therefore of concern to government, the education profession, health professionals and those concerned with all levels of competitive sports (grassroots to elite competitors).

The level, quality and standard of coaching and preparation for physical education become essential if the avoidance of risk of injury through inadequate input to the different disciplines is not understood and observed in the manner which has been forewarned throughout these pages.

APPENDIX 1

References

A Sporting Future for All, PP240, Department for Culture Media and Sport, 2000. Website: www.culture.gov.uk

New Opportunities Fund: is a lottery distribution body created by the **National Lottery Act 1998**. The Fund, which is a UK-wide non-departmental public body sponsored by the Department of Culture Media and Sport, is responsible for distributing grants for health, education and environment initiatives determined by the Government.

Standards Fund: is a collection of specific grants designed to achieve improvement in education standards, particularly for literacy, numeracy, social inclusion and GCSE. Grants are paid to LEAs who are required to devolve most of the money to schools. For most grants, LEAs are asked to make a 50% contribution, although some grants require no additional funding from the LEA.

The Door Wherein I Went, (Lord) Quintin Hogg Hailsham, Collins, 1975.

A Sparrow's Flight — The Memoirs of Lord Hailsham, (Lord) Quintin Hogg Hailsham, Collins, 1990.

Derek Wyatt, MP (Labour), Sittingbourne and Sheppey.

Prudent for a Purpose: Building Opportunity and Security for All: Spending Review: New Public Spending Plans 2001–2004, CM 4807, The Stationary Office 2000.

"Bodyline" cricket series: reference to The Ashes Series (Australia v England), 1932–33.

Ethics Injuries and the Law in Sports Medicine, Edward Grayson, Butterworths, 1999.

Sport and the Law, Edward Grayson, 3rd Edition, Butterworths, 1999.

Guidance On First Aid For Schools — A Good Practice Guide, DfEE, 1998.

Supporting Pupils With Medical Needs — A Good Practice Guide, DfEE & DoH, 1996.

Caught in Court, J Scott, Andre Deutsch, 1989.

National Curriculum for England: information can be accessed via website: www.nc.uk.net

MORI & BMRB surveys: MORI telephone schools survey (104 primary;100 secondary) throughout England during June 2000 revealed that 97% of schools are now providing out of school hours learning activities. A survey of 547 pupils by the British Market Research Bureau (BMRB) found that 35% of children say that sport is their most popular out-of-school hours learning activity although it was more popular among boys (42%) than among girls (28%).

Safe Practice in Physical Education, British Association of Advisors and Lecturers in Physical Education (BAALPE), 1995.

More powers to combat abuses in high-level adolescent sport needed, Tim Harding, The Lancet Vol. 348:9042, 1996, reference to report by A Franck and H Olagnier, Médecine et Hygiène, Vol. 54: 1393-96, 1996.

Little Girls in Pretty Boxes : The Making and Breaking of Elite Gymnasts and Figure Skaters, Joan Ryan, Warner Books, 1996.

Health And Safety Of Pupils On Educational Visits, DfEE, 2000.

The Use of Sunscreen in Schools : a good practice guide, Health Education Authority, 1999. Website: www.wiredforhealth.gov.uk

The Protection of School Playing Fields, Circular 3/99, DfEE, 1999.

Playing field equipment. Football goals. Functional and safety requirements, BS EN 748:1996.

Safety in Swimming Pools, The Health and Safety Executive and The Sports Council, 1989.

National Study of the Eepidemiology of Exercise, The Sports Council, 1991.

Sports Injury Clinics, R Knill-Jones, British Journal of Sports Medicine, Vol 31, 1997.

Framework Directive: Health and Safety, 89/391/EEC, European Union, 1989.

Five Steps to Risk Assessment, INDG 163, Health and Safety Executive, 1998.

School Health and Safety Management: Records and Procedures, Croner.CCH Group Ltd, 2001 (first published 1994).

APPENDIX 2

Acts and Regulations

ACTS OF PARLIAMENT:

Physical Education and Training Act 1937
Education Act 1944
Recreational Charities Act 1958
Employer's Liability (Compulsory Insurance) Act 1969
Health and Safety at Work, etc Act 1974
Education Act 1981
Local Government Finance Act 1988
Activity Centres (Young Persons' Safety) Act 1995
Disability Discrimination Act 1996
Education Act 1996
Human Rights Act 1998
School Standards and Framework Act 1998
National Lottery Act 1998

STATUTORY INSTRUMENTS:

Workplace (Health, Safety and Welfare) Regulations 1992, SI No. 3004
Reporting of Injuries, Diseases and Dangerous Occurrences Regulations 1995, SI No. 3100
Adventure Activities Licensing Regulations 1996, SI No. 772
Construction (Health, Safety and Welfare) Regulations 1996, SI No. 1592
Employers Liability (Compulsory Insurance) Regulations 1998, SI No. 2573
Education (Teachers) (Amendment) Regulations 1998, SI No. 1584

Management of Health and Safety at Work Regulations 1999, SI No. 3242

Education (School Premises) Regulations 1999, SI No. 2

Control of Substances Hazardous to Health Regulations 1999, SI No. 437

APPENDIX 3

List of Cases

Affuto-Nartoy v Clarke and ILEA, 1984, The Times 9 February 1984
Anderton v Clwyd County Council
Barfoot v East Sussex County Council, 1939, (unreported)
Beamont v Surrey CC, 1968, 66 LGR 580, 112 SJ 704
Campbell and Cosans v UK
Casson v MOD, 1999, Bradford Telegraph, Yorkshire Post 1999
Clark v Bethnal Green Corp, 1939, 55 TLR 519
Condon v Basi 1985, 2 All ER 453
Donoghue v Stevenson
Gannon v Rotherham MBC, 1991, Halsbury's Monthly Review 91/1717
Gibbs v Barking Corporation, 1936, All ER 115
Gillmore v London County Council, 1938, 4 All ER 331, 55 TLR 95, 159 LT 615
Gower v Bromley London Borough Council
IRC v McMullan, 1980, A.C.I.
Jarvis v Hampshire County Council
Kershaw v Hampshire County Council, 1982, (unreported)
Langham v Governors of Wellingborough School and Fryer, 1932, 01 LKJB 513, 147 LT 91; 96 JP 236; 30 LGR 276
Moore v Hampshire CC, 1981, 80 LGR 481 C
Morrell v Owen 1993, The Times 14 December 1993
Phelps v The Mayor and Burgesses of the London Borough of Hillingdon (The Times 28 July 2000)
R v David Calton, 1998, Yorkshire Post 29 September 1998
R v Kite, Stoddart and OLL Ltd
Ralph v LCC, 1947, 63 TLR 546, CA, 111 JP 548
Smolden v Whitworth and Nolan, 1996, The Times 18 December 1996, CA
Tracey Moore v Redditch and Bromsgrove Gymnast Club, 1981, (unreported)

LIST OF CASES

Van Oppen v Clerk to the Bedford Charity Trustees, 1988, 3 All ER 389, CA
Williams v Eady in 1893
Williams v Rotherham LEA, 1998, The Times 6 August 1998

Addresses and Organisations

Adventure Activities Licensing Authority
17 Lambourne Crescent
Cardiff Business Park
Llanishen
Cardiff CF14 5GF
Tel: 029 20 755715
Fax: 029 20 755757
E-mail: info@aala.org

All England Netball Association Ltd
Netball House
9 Paynes Park
Hitchin
Hertfordshire SG5 1EH
Tel: 01462 442344
Fax: 01462 442343
E-mail: info@aena.co.uk

Badminton Association of England
National Badminton Centre
Bradwell Road
Loughton Lodge
Milton Keynes MK8 9LA
Tel: 01908 268400
Fax: 01908 268412
E-mail: enquiries@baofe.co.uk

ADDRESSES AND ORGANISATIONS

The British Amateur Rugby League Association
West Yorkshire House
4 New North Parade
Huddersfield
West Yorkshire HD1 5JP
Tel: 01484 544131
Fax: 01484 519985
E-mail: info@barla.org.uk

British Association of Advisers and Lecturers in Physical Education
20 The Rise
Hempstead
Gillingham
Kent ME7 3SS

British Association of Sport and Exercise Sciences (BASES)
114 Cardigan Road
Headingley
Leeds LS6 3BJ
Tel: 0113 289 1020

The British Olympic Association
1 Wandsworth Plain
London SW18 1EH
Tel: 020 8871 2677
Fax: 020 8871 9104
E-mail: boa@boa.org.uk

British Standards Institution (BSI)
Group Head Quarters
389 Chiswick High Road
London W4 4AL
Tel: 020 8996 9000
Fax: 020 8996 7400
E-mail: Info@bsi-global.com

Central Council of Physical Recreation
Francis House
Francis Street
London SW1P 1DE
Tel: 020 7828 3163
Fax: 020 7630 8820
E-mail: info@ccpr.org.uk

Charity Commission (London)
Harmsworth House
13-15 Bouverie Street
London EC4Y 8DP
Tel: 0870 333 0123
Fax : 020 7674 2300

Charity Commission (Liverpool)
20 Kings Parade
Queens Dock
Liverpool L3 4DQ
Tel: 0870 333 0123
Fax: 0151 703 1555

Charity Commission (Taunton)
Woodfield House
Tangier
Taunton
Somerset TA1 4BL
Tel: 0870 333 0123
Fax : 01823 345003

The Commonwealth Games (2002)
4th Floor, Heron House
Albert Square
Manchester M2 5HD
Tel: 0161 817 2002
Fax: 0161 817 2004
E-mail: info@manchester2002.org.uk

HM Customs and Excise
New King's Beam House
22 Upper Ground
London SE1 9PJ
Tel: 020 7620 1313

Department for Culture Media and Sport (DCMS)
2–6 Cockspur Street
London SW1Y 5DH
Tel: 020 7211 6200

ADDRESSES AND ORGANISATIONS

Department for Education and Employment (DfEE)
Sanctuary Buildings
Great Smith Street
London SW1P 3BT
Tel: 0870 000 2288
Fax: 01928 794248
E-mail: info@dfee.gov.uk

Department of the Environment, Transport and the Regions (DETR)
Eland House
Bressenden Place
London SW1E 5DU
Tel: 020 7944 3000

Department of Trade and Industry (DTI)
Enquiry Unit
1 Victoria Street
London SW1H 0ET
Tel: 020 7215 5000

England and Walkes Cricket Board
Lord's Cricket Ground
London NW8 8QZ
Tel: 020 7432 1200
Fax: 020 7286 5583

English Hockey
National Hockey Stadium
Silbury Boulevard
Milton Keynes MK9 1HA
Tel: 01908 544644
Fax: 01908 241106

Edward Grayson
9–12 Bell Yard
London WC2A 2LF
Tel: 020 7400 1800
Fax: 020 7404 1405

Federation Internationale de Football Association (FIFA)
FIFA House
PO Box 85
8030 Zürich
Switzerland

The Football Association
25 Soho Square
London W1D 4FA

General Teaching Council (Birmingham)
3rd Floor Cannon House
24 The Priory
Queensway
Birmingham B4 6BS
Tel: 0870 0010308
Fax: (0121) 345 0100

General Teaching Council (London)
344-354 Gray's Inn Road
London WC1X 8BP
Tel: 0870 0010308
Fax: (020) 7841 2909

Health and Safety Executive (HSE)
Books Orders
PO Box 1999
Sudbury
Suffolk CO10 2WA
Tel: 01787 881165
Fax: 01787 313995

Hextall Erskine Solicitors
28 Leman Street
London E1 8ER
Tel: 020 7488 1424
Fax: 020 7481 0232
E-mail: info@hextalls.com

ADDRESSES AND ORGANISATIONS

Independent Schools Information Service
Grosvenor Gardens House
35-37 Grosvenor Gardens
London SW1W 0BS
Tel: 020 7798 1500
Fax : 020 7798 1501
E-mail: national@isis.org.uk

The National Lottery
Tel: 0845 9 100 000

National Playing Fields Association
Stanley House
St Chad's Place
London WC1X 9HH
Tel: 020 7833 5360
Fax: 020 7833 5365
E-mail: npfa@npfa.co.uk

The National Rounders Association
55 Westland Gardens
Westfield
Sheffield S20 8ES
Tel: 0114 2480357
Fax: 08700 520396
E-mail rounders@nra-rounders.co.uk

New Opportunities Fund (Head Office)
Heron House
322 High Holborn
London WC1V 7PW
Tel: 0845 0000 121

New Opportunities Fund (Scotland)
2nd Floor Highlander House
58 Waterloo Street
Glasgow G2 7DA
Tel: 0845 0000 123

New Opportunities Fund (Northern Ireland)
3rd Floor 24 Linenhall Street
Belfast BT2 8BG
Tel: 0845 0000 124

New Opportunities Fund (Wales) Office:
13th Floor Capital Tower
Greyfriars Road
Cardiff CF10 3AG
Tel: 0845 0000 122

Professional Associaiton of Teachers (PAT)
2 St James' Court
Friar Gate
Derby DE1 1BT
Tel: 01332 372337
Fax: 01332 290310 / 292431

Professional Association of Teachers (Scotland) (PAT)
4/6 Oak Lane
Edinburgh EH12 6XH
Tel: 0131 317 8282
Fax: 0131 317 8111

Qualifications and Curriculum Authority (QCA)
83 Piccadilly
London W1J 8QA
Tel: 020 7509 5555
Fax: 020 7509 6666

Rugby Football Union (England)
Twickenham
Middlesex TW1 1DS
Tel: 020 8831 6551
Fax: 020 8892 9816

Scottish Rugby Union
Murrayfield
Edinburgh EH12 5PJ
Tel: 0131 346 5000
Fax: 0131 346 5001

ADDRESSES AND ORGANISATIONS

Sport England
16 Upper Woburn Place
London WC1H 0QP
Tel: 020 7273 1500
Fax: 020 7383 5740
E-mail: info@english.sports.gov.uk
Website: www.english.sports.gov.uk

UK Athletics
Athletics House
10 Harborne Road
Edgbaston
Birmingham B15 3AA
Tel : 0121 456 5098
Fax : 0121 456 8752

Welsh Rugby Union
Ground Floor
Hodge House
St. Mary's Street
Cardiff CF1 1DY
Tel: 01222 390111
Fax: 01222 781722

INDEX

Index entries are to page numbers.

P

Order Form — School Sports and the Law
Please fill in this form if you would like to order further copies of School Sports and the Law

1.	Details of order

I would like to order _____ copies of Croner's School Sports and the Law @ £16 per copy (£14.50 per copy plus, £1.50 ppa).

Discounts: buy 10+ and receive a 5% discount, 20+ and receive a 10% discount, 30+ and receive a 20% discount.

Books will be despatched with an invoice.

2.	Order details — please complete

Name:

Job title:

Company:

Address:

Postcode:

Telephone number: **Date:**

3.	Your signature:_____

4. Further information

If you would like to order other books from Croner.CCH, please tick:

❏ School Governor's Legal Guide, £30 (including ppa) Bound book, 200 pages.

❏ Teacher's Rights Duties and Responsibilites, £16 (including ppa). Bound Books, 150 pages.

5. How to order

■ Telephone Customers Services on 020 8247 1261, or
■ Fill in your details, fold in half, seal outside edges and post this reply paid device.

VDHVC

BUSINESS REPLY SERVICE
Licence No KT1332

Bernard Johnson
Croner.CCH Group Limited
145 London Road
Kingston upon Thames
Surrey
KT2 6BR